Barbara R. Rettig

Cataloging Made Easy

Cataloging Made Easy

How to Organize Your Congregation's Library

Ruth S. Smith

A CROSSROAD BOOK

The Seabury Press • New York

NOTE

The writing of this book was encouraged and authorized by the Church and Synagogue Library Association, an ecumenical association of persons and institutions dedicated to the development and improvement of library services for local religious congregations. With headquarters at PO Box 1130, Bryn Mawr, PA 19010, the association also issues guides, bibliographies, leaflets, and a bimonthly, official bulletin, Church and Synagogue Libraries.

1978
The Seabury Press
815 Second Avenue
New York, N.Y. 10017

Printed in the United States of America

Library of Congress Cataloging in Publication Data

Smith, Ruth S
   Cataloging made easy.

   "A Crossroad book."
   1. Cataloging. 2. Libraries, Church.
I. Title.
Z693.S55   025.3   78-16983
ISBN 0-8164-2191-9

Contents

Preface

When I was in library school, my cataloging teacher often returned our catalog card assignments with mistakes circled in red - a missing comma here or an improper spacing there. I despaired of ever getting it "right." Later, as a working reference librarian, I found that the format of the card was of little interest as long as the cataloger had been consistent. The information itself was the important thing. Further, a catalog that included popular subject terms (perhaps as cross references) was infinitely more helpful, because that was the way the patrons asked for material.

In the mid 1950s, when we gathered books from around the church to form a library at the Bethesda United Methodist Church (Bethesda, Maryland), another librarian, Frances Fox Swim, and myself set up the cataloging procedures. We chose simplified cataloging rules based on standard library practices. The procedures had to be easy for volunteer helpers to follow, and the catalog had to be easy for the congregation to use. Since I did most of the cataloging in those early years, I discovered that cataloging could be fun.

I assembled a step-by-step procedures manual for our volunteer staff. We shared these procedures with other libraries. I used it in teaching cataloging classes for church library workshops. Recently, it was updated and published as Cataloging Books Step by Step (Bryn Mawr, PA, Church and Synagogue Library Association, 1977). Yet, there was so much more to be said about cataloging that I started to write about some of the other material in those workshop classes.

I have tried to dispel the mystique that surrounds cataloging: that it is difficult, and too complicated for an untrained professional to do "right." I also have tried to inspire the volunteer librarian to visualize catalog-building as a mission - a means of leading workers and parishioners to available resources which will satisfy their need for information and inspiration. In support of this, I have included practical material on why we catalog (separating the apples from the oranges), how to organize a collection based on an individual congregation's needs, and what to do to encourage use of the catalog as a directory to the collection's contents. (An easy-to-use card catalog stimulates library use.) In all, I hope I have relayed some of my own enthusiasm for reaching people and helping them to help themselves.

This material was gathered from more than twenty years of working with our own church library, reading and writing about libraries, speaking at or attending conferences (such as those sponsored by the Church and Synagogue Library Association, Box 1130, Bryn Mawr, PA), leading workshops around the country, visiting libraries and communicating with other librarians.

I am grateful to Willard H. Watts for providing all the photographs unless otherwise noted.

Ruth S. Smith

1/ Aiming toward a Library Ministry

"I need a book...I haven't much time."

Slightly breathless, a young Sunday school teacher on her way to a class of pre-schoolers continued, "It's red...about this big... on wearing warm clothing in winter. Can you find it?"

The librarian came to attention. "Don't you remember the name of it, or the author? Is it a children's book?"

"It's a children's book," the teacher gushed, "and I only remember that I have used it once before. It's a book with a lot of pictures and not much text."

"Let's look," the librarian said, springing into action. "Most of the picture books are on those shelves. You look there while I check the card catalog."

The catalog is an important tool. It is the only index to the collection which tells where on the shelf the materials are located. When you need to find items in a hurry, you find out how well you have built it. Each search is a test. Each test gives you insight into what the people are asking for and how they are asking for it. Add the information that will be helpful another time, if that information is not already in the catalog.

This librarian first looked under CLOTHING, found nothing, and then checked under WINTER. Sure enough, several books were listed - all juvenile fiction titles. The librarian hurried over to the shelf saying, "Let's try one of these." They found the books, arranged alphabetically by author. More than one of them had pictures on children playing outdoors in winter.

Would you have thought of putting a subject card into the catalog for a picture book? This cataloger did and, therefore, was able to find it. More than likely similar material had been asked for before.

Preparing to Be of Service

Ministry means reaching out to people and helping them. In a library or resource center this is done in many ways. One of those ways is the catalog. It guides and directs people to the resources that can answer their needs. A poorly conceived catalog is not much help. A catalog built for the use of the people is a surrogate for the trusted and experienced librarian - whether or not the latter is there to help.

In order to create this kind of catalog, you must be familiar with the people and their programs, be aware of the purpose and limits of your library service, and know what resources are available.

Be familiar with people and their programs.

Getting to Know the People

Each congregation is unique. Although people have predictable interests at various ages in life, they have differing backgrounds, reading and comprehension abilities, and program or problem needs. More about the interests of people at various ages can be found in Getting the Books Off the Shelves; Making the Most of Your Congregation's Library (New York, Hawthorn Books, 1975).

Seek to discover what makes your congregation special. What are the abilities and interests of the people you hope to serve? Find out what makes them tick. Talk with individuals about their work areas, study program or spiritual life. Look through back issues of the newsletter and the worship bulletin. Scan the book cards to see what books have circulated and to whom. Listen to the sermons. Talk with

3

the minister about future topics, special emphases, and concerns of
the congregation. Review regularly the official calendar of events.
Talk with the leaders. Mingle and talk with people at the coffee
hours and other events. Listen to the language they use. How do
they ask questions when they come into the library?

Store information about the congregation, such as unique words
and phrases they use. Keep a card file of these terms, for reference
use in cataloging. Collect information about the subjects of books
and other resources they like or need to use for current and future
curriculum studies or discussions. Note the subjects in which you
could use more material.

Selecting User-Oriented Resources

Cataloging begins with the selection process. Go through selected booklists, publishers' catalogs and curriculum guides and note
that they often are grouped by subject. For example, the Cokesbury
catalog of Religious Books 1976-77 grouped books under the following
topics:

Life-times of Faith (biographies)

Prayers and Devotions (specific prayers and daily meditations)

Christmas and Gift Books (holidays, celebrations and good books)

Understanding Ourselves and Others (mature living, self-disci-
   pline, loneliness, growing up, etc.)

To Grow in Faith (Christian responsibility, stewardship, belief,
   evangelism, medical ethics, growing spiritually)

4

Bibles and Bible Reference Books (versions, introductions, dictionaries, etc.)

Especially for Evangelicals (evangelical heritage and other books with this view)

Inspiration (Christian living, seasons of life, love and faith, joy of a God-filled life)

Favorites from 1975-76 (best-seller list)

Interpreting Our Faith (Holy Spirit, charismatics, theology, women in the church, church history, religions)

For You and Your Church (religious meaning, the church today, tithing)

Music and Worship Resources (songbooks, hymnals, forms of worship, weddings)

Christian Education (child study, retreats, parents, teaching aids)

Group Study Books (books for possible studies on prayer, crime, love, etc.)

The Minister's Shelf - Preaching (communication, quick quotes, gospel, sermons, manuals for funerals, marriage, etc.)

The Minister's Shelf - Counseling and Administration (problems, human pain, grief, tax records, pastoral care)

Children's Books (age group noted for each entry)

Look over your list of needed material to have it fresh in mind when you begin to select new books and other resources. Keep a pencil and pad of paper handy. Write down the title of a selected item, along with a word or two about who would be expected to use it and the subject area it would enrich.

If you are browsing among exhibits at a library workshop or in your favorite bookstore and buy the book on the spot, slip your note inside the cover for future reference. If you are placing an order, clip the slip to a copy of the order and keep it on file. This information will help to catalog the book when it comes in.

This approach to selection is a little like making out a shopping list before you go to the store. It tends to control the "impulse buying" of unnecessary material. From time to time most librarians purchase books for no reason other than that the books look attractive. For example, in our library we have several beautiful books which are admired but seldom (if ever) used. A person might exclaim, "Isn't that a beautiful book" - and then choose something else to take home. So be aware of the real needs of the congregation when you select material. Be familiar with the collection and nurture it in such a way that it will minister to these needs. Careful selection assures that the materials will be used. Enhance the subject areas of the library that are most actively in demand.

Dedicating Yourself to the Task

The most important element of building a library ministry is personal commitment. Along with a sincere desire to serve others, however, is the need for training and experience. Training comes from reading, talking and learning. Experience results from doing the work.

Read all you can about the church or synagogue, its work and
faith. Read all about libraries to become familiar with simple procedures based on standard library practice (See Appendix on Resources).
Visit other libraries and talk with librarians. Attend library workshops, such as those sponsored by local public libraries, councils
of churches or denominations. Plan to attend the annual conference
of the Church and Synagogue Library Association. Investigate library
courses offered by nearby community colleges or other schools. In-
quire about correspondence courses in congregational librarianship,
such as the one now offered by the University of Utah (Salt Lake City).

Remember that God is your partner. Communicate with Him often.
"Truly, Lord, You know I can't do this alone. I need Your help.
Guide me and direct my efforts, according to Thy will. Amen."

2/
Sorting the Collection

Much of life is a "sorting-out" process. Foods are separated on our dinner plate. Light clothes and dark clothes are divided in the wash. And there is the bride's side and the groom's side of the aisle at a wedding. One begins to learn this sorting-out process early in life. Some things are allowed and some things are not. The figurines in the side cabinet are not really toys, but the pots and pans in the cupboard are.

When I was a child growing up in the rural suburbs of Detroit, one of my favorite activities in the summertime was to play store. My sister and I - sometimes with a few friends - would go out and pick wild strawberries, thistles, "pickers," and the seeds of wild grasses that grew where houses had not yet been built. We collected these carefully and put them in separate boxes so they would not become mixed together. The boxes became "coffee," "tea," "berries," etc.

In the real world, store commodities are sorted in much the same way, and labeled. In a grocery store, the apples and oranges are separated in bins and marked with a price. In a department store, dresses and suits are sorted by size, tagged and placed on racks. In a library, books are classified by subject and labeled to give them a place on the shelf with other books of the same subject.

Toledo Public Library even sorts the trash (Photo by Toledo "Blade")

Bringing Order out of Chaos

Most church and synagogue libraries start out by collecting materials which have been purchased over a period of time for the various programs of the congregation, or by ordering a large batch of books - which arrive all at one time. New materials continue to arrive in no particular order. Until they can be sorted and arranged according to some logical scheme, only a very determined seeker will take the time to hunt through the disorder to find what he wants. It's a little like moving from one house to another. Inevitably, you find you need a hammer or an extension cord before the boxes are unpacked. Until things are sorted and stowed, the disorder can be discouraging.

When books first were gathered at Bethesda United Methodist Church to form a library, they were stowed side by side in no particular order in a glass-enclosed bookcase - just to get them together all in one place. I recorded the following: "Our first decision was to sort. Did we want to keep all those old books? The answer was no. Even though the collection was small, we wanted only new or attractive books that people would want to use. We separated the children's books from the adult books. Those we kept we arranged alphabetically by title until they could be cataloged and grouped by subject."

Arranging Material for Use

When a library has only a few books, the shelf arrangement might not seem important. One easily can look through the entire collection in a very short time and find what he wants. However, arrangement is vital to the use of the library as a collection grows - and grow it does. Our library grew from 83 books to 500 by the end of the first year, and had expanded to over 2,000 volumes within six years.

The initial arrangement, easy for the cataloger, is simply alphabetical by author or title. No decision is required about where the book "fits" in a subject classification scheme. The author and title usually are printed on the cover. It is easy to place or replace the book in its proper place on the shelf. Such an author-title arrangement will work well until the collection reaches about 500 volumes. Then, it becomes increasingly hard to find material on a subject by going to the shelves. Since most collections do grow beyond 500 volumes, it is wise to consider providing a subject arrangement and a subject index from the beginning.

A grouping of materials on the shelf by subject makes it easier for the library user to browse. A logical and systematic subject arrangement helps members of the congregation (as well as the library staff) to look for specific material that is needed. A collection that is easier for the patrons to use furthers the library's mission of ministry to individuals who search for information, inspiration and guidance.

In the simplest or the most complicated subject schemes, two basic decisions are made about a book when it is added to the collection: (a) what the book is about and (b) where you will shelve it in relation to other books in the collection. Whatever subject scheme you use,

11

these two decisions must be made. This process is called classifying the book. The plan for arranging subjects on the shelf is called the classification scheme.

There are a variety of classification schemes in use. Some are self-developed schemes. Others are based on classification schemes developed by others and tested by time and use. The best arrangement is one that allows books to be added and interfiled without disturbing the basic overall classification scheme. When you select a scheme, make sure that it will be adequate for your library when the collection reaches its maximum growth. Use this scheme from the beginning.

For a library of up to 1,000 books, a reader-interest subject scheme will create a browsable collection. For a library any larger than that, a simple Dewey Decimal Classification is recommended.

Reader-interest scheme. In order to attract customers, bookstores display books under reader-interest topics such as SPORTS, MYSTERIES, RELIGION, HOBBIES, ETC. A library patron, like the bookstore customer, generally will respond to an arrangement that allows him to browse in his area of interest.

One often hears: "We're just a small library and we don't need a complicated classification scheme. We just take all the books on a subject and assign those to the same shelf." The shelf assignments are subjects which reflect current interests and programs. Sounds simple.

A church library with a self-developed reader-interest scheme

usually will select topics such as BIBLE, RELIGIOUS EDUCATION, INSPI-
RATIONAL READING, etc. As the collection grows, categories are added
to subdivide the collection even further, perhaps MISSIONS, FAMILY
LIFE, BIOGRAPHY, SCOUTING, HOLIDAYS, THE CHURCH, SOCIAL CONCERNS, etc.
The librarian soon finds that a number of books can logically be filed
under more than one of these topics. For example, a book on child
study will be "at home" under RELIGIOUS EDUCATION as well as FAMILY
LIFE. A choice must be made. As the number of topics grows, the job
of the classifier becomes more complicated. No longer is it simply
"we just take all the books on a subject and assign those to the same
shelf." Observation and experience indicate that reader-interest
schemes serve well only in small libraries or for special collections
in large ones.

Mrs. C. B. Drew, Director of Christian Education, First Congregational Church, Wayne, Michigan, describes a collection which grew from
26 books to 600 in twenty-six years: "Our shelves are divided into
the following categories, making it easy to find what you are looking
for: THE CHURCH, THE BIBLE, CHILDREN'S BOOKS, JUNIOR DIVISION, JUNIOR
HIGH AND SENIOR HIGH RESOURCES AND READING BOOKS, FICTION AND NARRA-
TIVES, and BOOKS FOR INSPIRATION AND MEDITATION. Our library shelves
also have magazine racks...school bulletins and other pamphlets that
can be picked up and taken home. We also maintain a shelf for a complete set of curriculum materials as well as our Scouting program."[1]

A small room next to the church library was converted into a library for pre-school children at Abington (Pennsylvania) Presbyterian

Church. Their librarian describes it as follows: "The program is designed to encourage all pre-school children...to choose a book or a
recording from those provided in their very own library room. Books
and recordings are grouped by subjects....Categories designated for
books are ANIMALS, BIBLE, FOLKLORE, HUMOR, GIRLS AND BOYS, HOLIDAYS,
LEARNING, NATURE, OCCUPATIONS, TRANSPORTATION, etc....Categories for
recordings are ANIMALS, BIBLE, FOLKLORE, MARCHES, PLAYTIME, SLEEPY-
TIME, LISTEN AND LEARN, MUSIC and others." [2]

If a small library is expected to grow beyond about 1,000 books,
it is well to consider - in advance - how the arrangement will expand.
A well-organized, pre-designed plan allows future expansion to develop
in a natural and easy manner.

A church in Connecticut started out using a simplified subject
scheme recommended in one of the church library manuals. By the time
their collection reached 2,000 volumes, they decided it was inadequate.
They began to recatalog the entire collection using Dewey.

Maryann J. Dotts advises: "It will be necessary to decide on
some system of classification for new libraries. There are several,
and some churches have developed their own system. The Dewey Decimal
Classification System is a widely known system and is recommended for
the church resource library." [3]

The Riverdale Avenue Christian Church, Jacksonville, Florida,
adopted the Dewey scheme because "this is a method of classification
which is popular in small libraries of all kinds throughout the coun-

14

try."[4]

<u>Dewey Decimal Classification</u>. A scheme which combines the reader-interest concept with a logical subject order is the Dewey Decimal Classification. It places like material together and related subjects nearby. Material can be added and interfiled without disturbing the overall arrangement. It can be used in a simple form and expanded at a later date, as the need arises. The Dewey scheme is used in most school and public libraries. Therefore, it is familiar to people in general. This makes them feel at home with it in the church or synagogue library.

In 1873, while a college student of 21 at Amherst, Melvil Dewey worked out a scheme to divide all knowledge into ten basic classes. As the story goes, he imagined himself to be a prehistoric or primitive man. He asked himself the questions which he thought such a man would have asked. These questions formed the basis for nine of the classes. The tenth was reserved for topics so general they would not fall into any of the others. Then, as a shortened code, he assigned numbers from 0 through 9 to represent each. The nine basic classes are as follows:

Who am I?

100 - PHILOSOPHY AND PSYCHOLOGY

Who made me?

200 - RELIGION

Who is the man in the next cave?

300 - SOCIAL SCIENCES

15

How can I make that man understand me?

   400 - PHILOLOGY (LANGUAGE)

How can I understand nature and the world about me?

   500 - SCIENCE

How can I use what I know about nature?

   600 - APPLIED SCIENCE (TECHNOLOGY)

How can I enjoy my leisure time?

   700 - FINE ARTS, RECREATION

How can I give to my children a record of man's heroic deeds?

   800 - LITERATURE

How can I leave a record for men of the future?

   900 - HISTORY, GEOGRAPHY, BIOGRAPHY

000 - GENERAL WORKS is for books that do not fall into any specific subject category because they include information on many topics.
Shelve here the general encyclopedias, atlases, almanacs, etc.

100 - PHILOSOPHY AND PSYCHOLOGY includes metaphysical theories,
branches of psychology and pseudo psychology, and philosophical theories. Shelve here your books on existentialism, the nature of being,
healing of persons, mental illness, occult sciences, child study, ado-
lescence, aging, retirement, personality, idealism and hope for man.

200 - RELIGION includes theology, the Bible, doctrinal and devotional literature, pastoral and parochial concerns, the church, church
history, denominations and sects, and non-Christian religions. This
will be the largest class in a church or synagogue library. More will

be said about it later.

300 - SOCIAL SCIENCE includes political science, economics, law, social welfare, education, public services, and customs and folklore. Shelve here your books on church and state, refugees, politics, labor conditions, conservation of natural resources, canon law, social security, correctional institutions, teaching (except religious education), transportation, etiquette and woman.

400 - PHILOLOGY (LANGUAGE) includes texts and collections about language. Shelve here your Webster's dictionary, books of synonyms and antonyms, and texts for learning English (or Spanish or French, etc.).

500 - PURE SCIENCE includes mathematics, astronomy and allied sciences, physics, earth sciences, anthropology, biology, botany, and zoology. Shelve here the books on the solar system, dinosaurs, evolution of man, plants, seeds, trees, animals and birds.

600 - APPLIED SCIENCE (TECHNOLOGY) includes medical science, engineering, agriculture, home economics and chemical technology. Shelve here books on hygiene, railroads, flight, farms, forestry, domestic animals, food, child care and home nursing.

700 - FINE ARTS AND RECREATION includes architecture, sculpture, drawing and decorative arts, painting, photography, music and recreation. Shelve here books on ecclesiastical buildings, residential dwellings, ceramic arts, handicraft, stained glass, religious paintings,

sacred music and hymns, holidays, hobbies, games and sports.

800 - LITERATURE includes poetry, drama, essays, satire and humor
of various countries. Shelve here the collections of church plays,
poetry and cartoons.

900 - HISTORY, GEOGRAPHY, BIOGRAPHY includes the history of civil-
ization, geography and travel, biography, and history of major geographical areas of the world. Shelve here books on description and
travel, collective biography of religious leaders (except Bible charac-
ters, which will be shelved with books on the Bible) and background
reading on countries in the mission studies.

Each of Dewey's main classes is subdivided into ten categories.
An example is the 200 - RELIGION class, which is subdivided as follows:
200 - RELIGION
  210 - NATURAL THEOLOGY
  220 - BIBLE
  230 - DOCTRINAL
  240 - DEVOTIONAL
  250 - PASTORAL, PAROCHIAL
  260 - CHURCH, INSTITUTIONS & WORK
  270 - CHURCH HISTORY
  280 - DENOMINATIONS & SECTS
  290 - NON-CHRISTIAN RELIGIONS

Each of these is further subdivided into ten categories. For this
subdivision of the 200 - RELIGION class, see the Appendix.

These subdivisions form a three-level subject hierarchy which goes from the general to the more specific. You may choose to use the more general terms or you may use any or all of the subdivisions. When a subdivision is not used, all the books in that subject automatically collect under the more general heading. This is the basic Dewey scheme. In most cases, the basic scheme will adequately classify a church library collection. If needed, however, Dewey provides for further subdivisions.

Most people do not know why this scheme is called the Dewey _Decimal_ Classification. Dewey places a decimal point after the first three numbers. The subdivisions that follow no longer are in groups of ten. Further divisions are tailored to the individual needs of the subjects to be divided. The numbers after the decimal may be used, lopped off in the middle, or omitted altogether.

As material collects in certain subject areas, an expansion beyond the decimal may well be desired. For example, the Heights Christian Church in Houston, Texas, found it was useful to subdivide the 266 - MISSIONS classification by using numbers from the 900 - HISTORY class to identify the countries, as follows:

266.4 MISSIONS - EUROPE

266.5 MISSIONS - ASIA

266.6 MISSIONS - AFRICA

266.7 MISSIONS - NORTH AMERICA

266.8 MISSIONS - SOUTH AMERICA

266.9 MISSIONS - OTHER PARTS OF THE WORLD [5]

The ease with which Dewey can be expanded or simplified makes it ideal for church libraries. The same system will accommodate a small collection in certain subject areas and yet be adequate for a large collection in other subject areas - all within the same library. For example, a book about Mary, mother of Jesus, can be classified and shelved under any of the following numbers, depending upon how many books you have on Jesus Christ and how far you wish to subdivide the basic number:

232   JESUS CHRIST, CHRISTOLOGY

232.9   LIVES OF CHRIST

232.93 HOLY FAMILY

232.931 MARY

Esther J. Piercy says: "For the inexperienced classifier the danger is in being too specific. It is wasted effort and only confusing to use the most specific (longest) number for each book in a small collection.... The suggested numbers on Library of Congress cards usually need to be shortened. The classifiers at LC deliberately carry numbers to the farthest possible subdivision, taking it for granted that individual libraries will cut them to suit their needs." [6]

Groups of books, such as fiction, juvenile books and biography, are given the most general numbers or are handled ouside the Dewey scheme altogether. For example, "F" for fiction, "J" for juvenile fiction and "B" for individual biography. Sometimes adult fiction is not classed at all, but merely filed alphabetically by author on a shelf set aside for fiction. Then, in order to differentiate between

the adult and juvenile collections of non-fiction, a small "j" is
used before the class number of children's books: j225, jB.

Chances are you will never need the fullest expansion of a Dewey
class - even in the RELIGION section. The unabridged edition (now in
several volumes) is available for reference use in most public libraries. Instead, you will want to purchase the one-volume abridged
edition: Abridged Dewey Decimal Classification and Relative Index,
10th ed. (Albany, NY, Forest Press, 1971). Be sure to read the introduction carefully before you begin so you will be familiar with how
to make the most of it.

You might also wish to purchase the unabridged version of the
200 - RELIGION class, published as a separate pamphlet: Two Hundred
Religion Class, Dewey Decimal Classification (Nashville, TN, Broadman
Press, 1966).

Another useful aid which was prepared especially for congregational librarians is Classifying Church or Synagogue Library Materials by
Dorothy B. Kersten (Bryn Mawr, PA, Church and Synagogue Library Association, 1977). Based on the Dewey system, the classifications suggested cover subjects which would most likely be found in these libraries. A companion volume is Subject Headings for Church or Synagogue
Libraries by Dorothy B. Kersten (same publisher).

Then, to round off your set of cataloging tools, obtain the standard list of subject headings which is based on the Dewey scheme: Sears
List of Subject Headings, edited by Barbara M. Westby, 10th ed. (Bronx,

21

NY, H. W. Wilson Co., 1972).

Library of Congress scheme. When the library of Thomas Jefferson - a collection of some three million books - was given to the Library of Congress in 1915, they began with the classification he used and developed a scheme to reclassify and recatalog the entire collection. This scheme provides for minute groupings of subjects and is used today in many large, scholarly and technical libraries. Greatly simplified versions of it have been developed by individual church libraries, but there is no standard, simplified LC scheme. It was not meant to be simplified.

The LC system divides all knowledge into twenty-one classes. These classes are identified by a code composed of letters of the alphabet. Subclasses are represented by combinations of letters. Subtopics within classes and subclasses are identified by numbers. The main classes are, as follows:

A   GENERAL WORKS: POLYGRAPHY

B   PHILOSOPHY AND RELIGION

        PART I, B-BJ: PHILOSOPHY

        PART II, BL-BX: RELIGION

C   HISTORY: AUXILIARY SCIENCES

D   HISTORY: GENERAL AND OLD WORLD

E-F   HISTORY: AMERICA

G   GEOGRAPHY, ANTHROPOLOGY, FOLKLORE, etc.

H.   SOCIAL SCIENCES

J   POLITICAL SCIENCE

K   LAW

L   EDUCATION

M   MUSIC

N   FINE ARTS

P   PHILOLOGY AND LITERATURE

Q   SCIENCE

R   MEDICINE

S   AGRICULTURE, etc.

T   TECHNOLOGY

U   MILITARY SCIENCE

V   NAVAL SCIENCE

Z   BIBLIOGRAPHY AND LIBRARY SCIENCE

In this scheme, the letters I, O, W, X and Y were left for future expansion. Biography in general is classified with C - HISTORY: AUXILIARY SCIENCES. The lives of individuals which are illustrative of any subject are classified with that subject.

The first subdivision of the RELIGION category is as follows:

    BL RELIGIONS, MYTHOLOGY, RATIONALISM

    BM JUDAISM

    BP ISLAM, BAHAISM, THEOSOPHY, etc.

    BR CHRISTIANITY

    BS BIBLE

    BT DOCTRINAL THEOLOGY

    BV PRACTICAL THEOLOGY

    BX DENOMINATIONS AND SECTS

23

The subcategory BIBLE is divided into nearly three thousand subtopics. Of these, 356 numbers relate to texts and versions, 1,129 numbers are related to the Old Testament and 1,069 the New Testament.

The unabridged LC Classification Schedule occupies approximately two feet of shelf space. The volume of subject headings which the Library of Congress developed for this scheme is larger than the unabridged dictionary.

Weine classification. The lack of a satisfactory classification scheme for the average Jewish library led Mae Weine to devise a thirteen-page classification scheme for small Judaica libraries, such as one in a synagogue or school. In the preface to the sixth edition she says: "Although based upon the Dewey system, certain areas have been drastically revised, most notably in the fields of religion, Jewish education, and history. In every case, whether or not explicitly stated, the number refers only to the Jewish aspect of the subject in question. Since the scheme is intended only for Judaica collections, the letter 'z' has been added throughout, to distinguish it from the regular Dewey system. This will be useful in the case of libraries with 'mixed' collections, i.e., containing books of a general as well as of a Jewish nature." [7]

Identifying locations. When worship services were over, I went to the library out of habit, to browse. A lady came in and stood looking bewildered. The librarian was busy. "Need some help?" I offered.

24

"Well," she hesitated. "I thought I might get me a book...something light...artsy-craftsy maybe...just something to keep me out of mischief."

"The newer books are in a rack on top of the card catalog," I explained, walking toward it with her. I selected one from the rack and handed it to her. "Have you read Norma? It is the biography of Norma Zimmer and people who have read it say it is very good." She accepted it uncertainly. "The adult books are all along this wall, with biography around the corner," I continued. "Fiction is in the first section near the door. Then the subjects range from philosophy and religion to the arts, literature and history." I reached for a book in the literature section. "You might like one of Gladys Tabor's books," I said, "they are filled with charming reminiscences of life in New England."

She took the book. As she leafed through it her eyes brightened. "It has brief chapters, too," she observed, "so you could set it down and pick it up again later." She tucked it in the crook of her arm, along with the other book already there.

I started to tell her about two other books on the shelf in similar vein, but she really wasn't listening anymore. Something had caught her eye in an adjacent section. She reached for I'm OK, You're OK by Thomas Harris and said, "I've heard so much about this book, I had better find out what it is all about." Then, with that secret smile of a satisfied customer, she thanked me, charged out all three

25

books and went off with a lilt in her step. More than likely the next time she visits the library she will return to the same sections to make a selection.

Explain the arrangement.

In the absence of someone who can guide a reader to the locations of materials, good identification of layout is needed.

General layout. Look first at your library layout. Are the furnishings inviting and the location of material convenient for the intended customers? Sylvia Cox, Librarian of St. Pius X Library at the Shrine of the Most Blessed Sacrament in Washington, D. C., explains their library layout as follows:

We have the use of what was once the living room of

a private residence and an addition running across the whole rear of the home.

The front room...with its fireplace and comfortable sofa and chairs has a gracious and homelike air, which seems to be conducive to pleasant group discussion and relaxing reading. Children in particular seem to enjoy settling down on the sofa and reading to each other near our growing collection of books for them. Fiction and quite a large section devoted to homemaking occupy the rest of the shelf space.

The back room...opening on a spacious lot that serves the Church, the Convent, the School and an activities building temporarily serving as a community building for the Chevy Chase area, is more purely utilitarian in atmosphere. Here are the sections for reference, religion, literature, sociology, fine arts, psychology, philosophy, education, biography, history, travel, science, and a Latin American collection...The library contains 5,000 volumes. There are also most of the current Catholic magazines, as well as periodicals like the Saturday Review displayed....

Serious research is one more service the Library offers both to scholarly priests and general readers. Braille books are available. There are special

shelves for Boy Scout materials and for Confraternity
of Christian Doctrine teachers. A small collection of
children's books are arriving from Spain for the bene-
fit of a large colony of Spanish-speaking parishioners....[8]

As our own library collection grew, we were fortunate enough to
be able to move the library to a new location. The children's corner
was located just inside the door, on one side. On the other was periodical shelving and fiction, preceding the Dewey classes of non-
fiction. Special shelves or file cabinets were provided for reference
books, college catalogs, pictures/pamphlets/clippings, filmstrips,
games, teaching kits and other special materials.

Special shelves are reserved for specific purposes at the Grace
United Presbyterian Church, Council Bluffs, Iowa:

Women's society shelf, with the current recommended reading.

Mission study shelf, with open files containing folders of
magazine articles, profiles, pictures, and pamphlets on
mission work and personnel, filed according to geographic
area.

Scrapbook shelf, with early pictures, programs, news clippings,
old minutes (found in attics and storerooms), and current
material collected as things happen.

College shelf, with a loose-leaf notebook of available material
on careers, information on church-related schools, colleges

and universities, and paperback books about going to college, summer jobs, etc.[9]

Sections of shelves. As you walk into your own library, is the
content of the various sections easily identified? If you have set
aside special collections for specific purposes, are you capitalizing
on this special service, or is it "lost"? Labeling helps. However,
signs on sections or shelves must be clearly legible and distinctive
enough to attract attention. Make them stand out from the background
- either in format or in content.

Color attracts attention. It can be used effectively as an aid
to identification. Joyce L. White suggests a "color-coded Dewey."
She explains as follows: "Several years ago I was helping the staff
of a small library recatalog from a homemade scheme that the collection had outgrown....Initially, each of the ten basic Dewey subject
areas was assigned a color. Secondly, all the subject divisions were
thought of within the field of religion - as distinct from 'religion'
being only one of the subjects among the ten. Immediately, therefore,
the whole Dewey schedule was available to us for use and not just the
categories within the 200 class as would ordinarily have been the
case. Thirdly, we sorted all the books by putting colored tape across
the spine and making a colored stripe along the top of the correspond-
ing catalog card with a felt tip pen of matching color. In our scheme,
blue was assigned to 'religion' and further subdivided into three
sections identified by the shades of light, royal and navy blue.

Color-Coded Dewey Classification

Color	Dewey Classification
TAN	PHILOSOPHY (100)
BLUE	RELIGION (200)
Light Blue	Devotions, prayer, worship
Royal Blue	Doctrines, beliefs, creeds
Navy Blue	Bibles, commentaries, studies
RED	SOCIAL SCIENCES (300) (include religious education with education)
PINK	LANGUAGE (400)
PURPLE	SCIENCE (500) (include issues of science and religion)
ORANGE	TECHNOLOGY (600)
YELLOW	FINE ARTS (700) (include hymns and church music)
GREEN	LITERATURE (include religious classics)
BROWN	HISTORY (900) (include Church history)
BLACK	GENERAL (000) (include religious bibliographies and periodicals)

Mark books by using strips of colored tape across the spine.
Mark catalog cards with felt-tip pen of matching color across top of card or purchase color-banded cards.

"We found that by placing the books on the shelves by their color grouping in author sequence, that with only a two-letter signal for the author's last name, all the books could be easily located, and the library remained open and in use during the whole reclassification procedure.

"It was obvious, however, that for a small library between 300
and 500 books, the color coding is all the classification that is actually needed. For those volunteers just starting libraries in par-
ishes where none has previously existed, the scheme provides a system
of organization that lends itself to growth. The basic structure of
the Dewey Decimal Classification is therefore established right at the
beginning so that numbers can be easily assigned as time goes on and
the collection expands. Furthermore it is not necessary at the later
date to remove the colored tape, but simply place numbers on it thus
helping easily to identify books for handy reshelving."[10]

At our church, we once experimented with the use of color coding
to designate age groups within the children's section of books. A
narrow piece of colored mystic tape was affixed to the spine of the
book just below the label. A colored pencil was used to place a matching dot on the book card and pocket. We ran into difficulty because
the slow readers objected to selecting books meant for younger ages
and the teachers never seemed to remember which color was which. We
eventually abandoned the scheme and installed brightly colored shelf
markers to identify juvenile fiction, youth fiction and various subjects
of non-fiction.

Color was used by the Information Center on Children's Cultures
(a division of the U. S. Committee for UNICEF) to arrange a collection
of materials about children in the developing countries. Janie Filstrup explains it as follows: "Each item in the collection is placed
in one of ten color-coded geographical areas....The assigned color band

31

goes across the top of each catalog card...and on the spine of the book or in some conspicuous place on other media." The purpose of using this "rainbow of a catalog" is to find materials as easily as possible in terms of large world areas, to provide quick visual identification as to the general contents and to allow for easy selection of material on the shelves. [11]

Material on shelves. Label the materials as well as the sections and shelves. Then, when a book is taken off a shelf, it will be simple to get it back to its proper place. Without a symbol to identify its shelf assignment, you will find yourself "re-classifying" the book each time it is replaced.

An old Chinese proverb says a picture is worth a thousand words. A graphic symbol or code to represent the idea of a subject takes up less space, is easy to see and can be recognized at a glance. For example, symbolic street signs are being used in many cities today to identify pedestrian crosswalks, wheelchair ramps, bicycle paths and forbidden turns. As people travel around from place to place they recognize and easily interpret these standard signs.

Symbols that represent subjects or locations for books and other materials serve much the same purpose in a library. They are roadsigns that direct the "pedestrians" who "travel" that way. These symbols might be standard abbreviations for words, colors, pictures, numbers, letters - or a combination of these.

Abbreviations quite often are used to identify special collections.

For example, "R" or "Ref." is used as a symbol for books that do not circulate but remain on the shelf for reference use in the library. "J" or "Juv." often is used to identify juvenile books.

Colors effectively describe certain categories of books, as pointed out earlier. Just a piece of tape, a colored dot sticker or a light daub of fingernail polish on the spine of a book takes on meaning. Post a key to the colors nearby for reference.

Pictures also have been used to identify broad categories of books. They are used in some public libraries and hospital patients' libraries to call attention to mystery stories or westerns. Try drawing your own symbolized pictures to represent various subjects. Space these properly on a sheet of paper and photocopy your designs on sheets of self-adhesive labels. Most printers will "print" labels from camera-ready copy. If you ask the printer to help with preparing the sketches, it will cost more, but many are willing to do this. An alternative is to have a rubber stamp made to order for each symbol.

Classification symbol labels for easy picture books are available in convenient self-dispensing boxes.

Numerals or letters of the alphabet - or a combination - are standard call numbers. They are short, easy to inscribe and easy to see. Piercy says that if the symbol is a subject classification number, it "serves two purposes: it locates a specific work and it brings it together with like materials. The user is led to the desired specific book, or he may browse through books on the shelf which relate to the subject in which he is interested." [12]

A call number is composed of the subject number with an author symbol. The author symbol gives the book a more specific place on the shelf within a classification number. This call number is recorded in the book, on the book (spine label) and on all catalog cards that describe the book. It is like an address. The subject class number is the name of the street and the author symbol is the house number.

Author symbols for church and synagogue library collections usually are quite simple. They consist of the first letter of the author's last name, plus one or two other letters that follow it. To distinguish between more than one book written by the same author, sometimes the first letter of the title also is added. In the case of biography, the name of the person about whom the book is written forms the author symbol and the first letter of the author's name is added to it - to distinguish between biographies of the same person written by different authors. In all cases, if the call number thus formed has already been used to identify another book, alter the letters after the first one just enough to make the call number unique. After the first letter of the author's last name, the others selected need not be exactly as they appear consecutively in the spelling of the name.

Public libraries, because of their size and need for expanded author schedules, use the Cutter Number Tables. These tables provide
numbers after the first letter of English language names to give them
an alphabetical sequence. They are available for purchase from H. R.
Huntting Company, Inc., 300 Burnett Road, Cicoppe, MA 01020.

Each item to be shelved has a label on which the call number is
inscribed. Make sure this label is clearly visible. On books, it
generally appears on the spine of the book near the bottom. Measure
a predetermined distance up from the bottom of the book to mark the
bottom of the label. Labels that form a straight line across the
shelf are easier for the user to scan. They create a neater look for
the shelf as well.

Labels can be written on the spine of a cloth book by using an
electric stylus and transfer paper. The electric stylus is similar
to one found in a child's woodburning set. The transfer paper comes in
different colors. White is recommended for writing on dark bindings
and black for the light ones.

Plain labels, available from library supply houses, are meant to
be lettered and pasted on the book. Among the pressure-sensitive types
(simply peel off to apply) are heavy-duty fabric labels, paper labels
and some with extra tacky adhesive. (Labels will be described further
in Chapter 4.)

When inscribing the call number on the label, use a large-print typewriter, if one is available. If hand lettering is to be done, use a permanent black ink and a firm stroke with even spacing for good visibility. Remember, neatness counts.

Be imaginative in lettering directional signs and shelf markers, but try to keep the labels on books and other materials as neat, legible and uniform as possible.

3/ Establishing Cataloging Guidelines

When my son was growing up, his grandmother would come to visit us for a month each summer. She was much loved and her visit was anticipated with pleasure. However, the effort on her part required some adjustment. She had difficulty seeing. New locations or rearranged furniture were confusing until she became familiar with their relative locations. In order to help her, my husband fastened a light weight rope from one corner of her bed to a large chair by the door, through the hallway, to a small bath nearby. This was her "guide" line until she became confident. More than likely she could have found her way around without it, but it was reassuring to her. With a touch it told her that she was safely on the right track and going in the right direction.

A volunteer library staff tends to be transient and often finds itself "in the dark" about established policies and procedures. Guidelines become very important. They set you on the right track and keep you going in the direction of previously established goals and objectives. That alone is reassuring.

Setting Goals and Defining Limits

Guidelines for cataloging are especially important. Yet they are of no importance unless they are attached to a goal. In other words, they must lead somewhere. They also must define how far afield it is safe to stray in getting there.

<u>Review the purpose</u>. What is the purpose of a catalog? Just as the classification system establishes an arrangement for the books on the shelf, the process of cataloging produces a catalog. The catalog - usually on cards - helps to determine whether or not a specific book is in the collection and where on the shelf to find it. Quite often these two activities - classifying and cataloging - are referred to simply as cataloging. This emphasizes the importance of having a catalog as an end product -- an index to the resources.

"Classification and cataloging in a parish library should be accurate, simple, and useful," says Joyce L. White, past president of the Church and Synagogue Library Association. "Accurate in that the system is consistent and the work is done conscientiously. Simple, in that the system itself is not needlessly complicated by including information applicable only to large research libraries. And useful in that the classification and the cataloging that is done is directly relevant to the specific library for which it is designed to be used." [1]

Look back to the purposes of your library as a ministry. Think carefully about the people it hopes to serve. Choose a classification scheme that will be suited to their needs, be easy to use, and yet will allow for an organized and logical expansion as the collection grows. The catalog will list the material that is in the collection - books, parts of books or other material. It will direct the users to the location of this material on the shelf. Therefore, the format, scope and arrangement of the catalog itself must be carefully planned in advance so it will be easy to consult and will support the objectives of your library ministry.

Choose a format. A card catalog format is recommended. The drawers of a card catalog are lettered to indicate content. Guide cards within each drawer point out the locations of major headings. Therefore, a person can go almost directly to the information he seeks. Further, more than one person can use the catalog at any one time. Corrections can be made simply by removing a few catalog cards at a time. New additions can be interfiled. All this without disturbing the basic alphabetical arrangement.

A book catalog, like a ledger book, provides a more "permanent" record, but it is not as flexible. Corrections are not easy to make without damaging the entry. New additions are not interfiled, but must be tacked on at the end. An alphabetical arrangement of entries is impossible, except under the basic alphabetical letters. This, of course, assumes that the book catalog is being maintained manually -- by hand.

Book catalogs are coming into their own again with the advent of computers. Cataloging information is stored in the computer and updated catalogs are printed out at regular intervals. These are easy to reproduce. Therefore multiple copies of the catalog are available, so more than one patron can use it at any one time. Corrections are easy to make, because they are done within the computer. A corrected catalog is automatically arranged alphabetically by all the entry points. Some day, through cooperative library cataloging programs or through the use of individual mini-computers (which are becoming less expensive all the time), church and synagogue libraries will become automated. Can you imagine an up-to-date list of the library's holdings in the minister's office, in each church school department and in the lounge - as well as in the library itself? The possibility is not as far off as it seems.

Determine the scope. Whether prepared manually or automated, the important thing is what you put into the catalog. In its simplest form, the catalog is a listing by author, or author and title, to show what the library has. A "full-service" catalog contains other access points under which material can be found - subjects, joint authors, series, parts of books, etc.

Small libraries, generally, have greater need for entries which identify parts of books. For example, one or two religious plays in a general collection might be the only religious plays in the library. By including this kind of detailed entry - called analytics - the catalog can expand the potential use of the library's resources.

Review the library's size and subject coverage. Consider the questions that people ask when they come into the library. What do they need to find? How much information does the catalog have to supplement the shelf arrangement?

Alice F. Toomey says of the Washington Hebrew Congregation Library, Washington, D.C.: "The collection is being developed to provide a well-rounded resource for the adult members of the congregation in the fields of Judaism and the Jewish way of life. It includes basic source materials, such as the Torah, the Talmud, encyclopedias and Biblical concordances; Jewish history, customs, etc.; comparative religions; literature, art and biography; and the history and development of the State of Israel." [2] It also includes subject headings in the card catalog.

The shelf arrangement is the major subject key to the Mount Olivet Lutheran Church Library in Minneapolis. Erwin E. John describes the collection as follows: "For children, religious books are supplemented with many other wholesome books that are not of a strictly religious nature. For adults, the collection is generally restricted to books which relate directly to the Christian's vocation. But this may include (1) fiction which has religious significance; (2) literature, poetry, and drama which pertain to Christian values; (3) books of inspiration; (4) Christian biography; (5) devotional books; (6) works on worship, music and art; (7) books on the church in general, denominations and organizations; (8) books on theology and doctrine; (9) books about missions, both at home and abroad; (10) the Bible and books about it, including commentaries; (11) books dealing with morals and ethics, both individual and social; (12) books in the field of psychology and education, including teachers' helps; (13) books dealing with personal problems and social welfare, such as alcoholism, mental health, and delinquency; (14) books on religious history, philosophy, and world religions and (15) travel and geography books, including atlases." These categories make up the classification scheme. Books are arranged alphabetically by author under each main category. [3]

Broad subject terms on the shelf are helpful. Specific subject terms can supplement these in the catalog - terms such as finger plays, stained glass and circuit riders.

The more ways in which you are able to look up material in the catalog, the better are your chances of finding answers to user inquiries. Keep track of the questions that people ask. This will help to identify weak spots in the subject collection and will also give you ideas for making improvements in the catalog. Questions that were asked over a period of years at the Bethesda United Methodist Church include the following (Sears subject headings have been added after each to show where material might have been listed in the catalog):

Material appropriate for junior mission studies (MISSIONS - divided by country)

Colored flags of all nations (FLAGS)

Books to help identify insects (INSECTS)

Material on migrant workers, for children (MIGRANT LABOR)

Devotional books (DEVOTIONAL LITERATURE)

Church affiliated schools and colleges (COLLEGES AND UNIVERSITIES; SCHOOLS)

Pictures of Christ (JESUS CHRIST - ART; CHRISTIAN ART AND SYMBOLISM)

Going to church, for sixth grade (WORSHIP; CHURCH ATTENDANCE see WORSHIP)

Summer camps (CAMPING)

Early days of the church (CHURCH HISTORY)

Service of installation of officers (RITES AND CEREMONIES)

Saint Paul (PAUL, SAINT)

Pictures and stories of the apostles (APOSTLES)

Rousing songs for Bible school (SCHOOL SONG BOOKS)

Who were Jesus' brothers? (JESUS CHRIST - BIOGRAPHY)

Subject entries in the catalog supplement the shelf arrangement in other ways, too. For example, Gertrude Ackermann Ogden explains: "Author and title cards for most of the books in the library were typed first, but not a single subject card was made. The library committee later decided that subject cards would be very helpful for these reasons: first, persons not familiar with the classification system are apt to look under a subject heading to find the correct call number; and secondly, a book may cover two subjects and require two subject headings." [4]

Decide on the kind of service you will provide. How much information will you put into the card catalog to guide others in finding their own way? How much knowledgeable staff will be on hand to help users, or is this to be a self-service library much of the time? The answers to these questions should influence how much depth (detail) is needed in the catalog.

Catalog arrangement. How and where will the cards be filed? A catalog card cabinet made for the purpose is recommended. Each drawer should have a metal rod which holds the cards in place. If the drawer is dropped, the cards will remain locked in place. How the cards are filed also is important.

A divided catalog is one in which personal names (authors, joint authors, editors, translators, etc.) are filed in one alphabetical sequence. All title cards are filed together in their own alphabetical sequence. Subjects are filed together in still another. Catalog cards for audio-visual materials are filed apart from the card catalog for books. Filing into a divided catalog is easy for the one filing the cards. But, the searcher often has to go to more than one file to find what he wants.

A better arrangement for the user is an integrated card catalog. Cards for all materials in the library, including books, tapes, filmstrips, slides and other media, are filed in one alphabetical sequence, like a dictionary. Filing into the integrated catalog is a little more challenging. The word of an author's name, a title, and a subject can be the same word. However, there are simple rules that govern which is filed first. (See Chapter 6 for general filing rules.) The effort is well worth it because the searcher finds all material on a subject listed in one place.

Selecting a Cataloger

What makes a good cataloger? Three essential qualities are: attitude, expertise and faith - not necessarily in that order. In many church and synagogue libraries, the librarian also is the cataloger. So, this section is addressed to the librarian.

Adopt the proper attitude. Approach the job with the assurance that you can't _really_ make a mistake. All classification is a matter of judgment. If the first place you decide to locate an item turns out not to be useful, the classification can be changed. As long as the material can be located, your judgment is correct. Try to be consistent. This will tend to keep like materials together. If you find that additional entries are needed in the catalog, these easily can be added at any time. Good judgment in these matters grows with experience.

Basic requirements. As a cataloger, have a firm grounding in the faith. This is essential. A person needs to have an understanding of what it means to be a Christian (or a Jew) to catalog materials for others with these same beliefs. As a member of the congregation, you will become familiar with the programs and interests of this unique community. You will learn how to communicate - to relay information - in the language of the community.

Acquire expertise. Get the most out of your cataloging by being well prepared for it. Take time to become familiar with standard library procedures for doing the job right. Then, be consistent so others can follow what you have done.

One person should be responsible for the cataloging - to make sure that it is done according to the established policies and procedures. A person with a little enthusiasm, a background in the subject field, and a willingness to learn usually can pick up enough expertise to do an acceptable job, alone or with a team of helpers.

When Burke Avenue Chapel in Seattle established its library in 1962, Mrs. Edith Dietz, librarian, managed with a staff of three, a church library manual, a Sears subject heading list and a Dewey Decimal book. She tells the story as follows: "While the shelves were being built, and the Library being put into readiness, the books were pouring in. They were donated by friends and members of Burke Avenue Chapel and waiting to be processed. As I had no training or experience as a librarian I had much to learn.... With the help of Miss Marilyn Heiliger, our Christian Education Director, and a group of students from Seattle Pacific College, we set to work on 400 books and pamphlets, classifying, putting in book pockets, date slips, marking, typing catalog cards, and in every way, getting the books ready and on the shelf by Opening Night." Hers was the thrill of charging out the first book to be circulated. [5]

Dividing the work. Establish a work schedule. Check all work - including your own - before cards are filed or books are shelved. Accuracy is important. Consistency is essential.

If more than one person is to help with the cataloging, divide the responsibilities as follows:

Cataloger (one person)	Helpers (one or more)
	Open new book properly.
	Accession the book and affix ownership stamp.
	Check catalog to see if this is an added copy.

                              Make work card, copying the
                              author, title, publisher
                              and date from the book.

Check work card against the
    book, indicate corrections
    or additions.
Assign the classification
    number, checking authority
    files to be sure it is
    consistent with previous
    practice.
Assign a tentative author
    symbol and check the call
    number against the shelf
    list. Alter author symbol
    if necessary to form a
    unique number.
Assign subject headings and
    other added entries.

                              Type catalog cards, shelf
                              list card, book card and
                              pocket, and label for each
                              work card.

Check all typing for accuracy.

                              File catalog cards above rods.

Check filing and drop cards

into place in drawers.

> Prepare book for shelf --
>
> paste, letter, etc.
>
> Shelve book.

Keep statistics.

Some people prefer to work when the library is closed, so that these processes can be done without interruption. However, this is not always possible. Therefore, in order to accommodate irregular schedules (and take advantage of the time that people are available to work), set up a work cabinet. Label the shelves to indicate each step in the processing cycle. As one process is completed, place the material on the next shelf. Each worker will know immediately what needs to be done next: accessioning, classifying, labeling, etc. Some libraries assign specific workers to the various jobs. Each is assigned a shelf of work to be done.

The library committee of the First Lutheran Church, Ellicott City, Maryland, sets aside one morning each week for accessioning, cataloging and planning. [6]

Library Aides, a group of high-school girls, help with the processing of books at Christ Episcopal Church, Oil City, Pennsylvania. The president of the Library Aides describes their participation as follows:

> At each meeting a program is presented. We have seen
> films about storytelling, libraries and librarianship. We
> have previewed filmstrips which we might use in the summer

story hours. We give our own short book reviews. We discuss how to work in a library. Then there is a work session, followed by business and refreshments. In the work session, we add material to the pamphlet file, label subject headings on the folders, file catalog cards, make posters, prepare bulletin boards, shelve returned books and keep the circulation up to date.[7]

Opportunities to learn. Enthusiasm and knowledge of the faith are important, but they alone will not prepare you for the job. A grounding in the basics of cataloging is essential. Fortunately, there are opportunities to learn standard, simple library cataloging practices.

Obtain one of the general manuals for operating a church or synagogue library (see Appendix). These are helpful. They give an overview of recommended procedures. When you need a fuller explanation to solve a specific problem, seek out someone with more experience than yourself.

Visit other libraries. Talk with librarians. Exchange ideas. Since public libraries generally use the Dewey Decimal Classification scheme and maintain collections of religious books, public librarians can be especially helpful. Groups and associations, such as the Church Library Council in the Greater Washington, D.C., area and the Church and Synagogue Library Association (with its local chapters) provide opportunities for fellowship relationships to ripen into reliable advisory sources.

Attend library conferences and workshops. Councils of churches, bookstores and public libraries often sponsor church library workshops. The Sunday School Board of the Southern Baptist Convention (Church Library Department, 127 Ninth Avenue North, Nashville, TN 37203) and The United Methodist Church (Church Library Service, 201 Eighth Avenue South, Nashville, TN 37202) offer week-long library training sessions each year. The Church and Synagogue Library Association (Box 1130, Bryn Mawr, PA 19010) holds an annual conference (in a different city each year), publishes guides, and will respond to specific questions through personal correspondence.

Take courses at school. Community colleges often offer general library courses that are quite suitable. Certain colleges and universities are beginning to offer correspondence courses in congregational librarianship. One such is the University of Utah (Salt Lake City, UT 84112).

With the turnover of a volunteer staff, there generally will be a need for training and retraining. The Hawthorne, New Jersey, Gospel Church library solved this problem as follows: "For training, the recruit is paired with a committee member or another experienced staff member. By observing, assisting, and generally assuming responsibilities, she gains expertise and confidence until both on the team decide it is time to go it alone.... Staff and group meetings, individual tutoring, and journals provide in-service training." Each volunteer is given the Library Handbook, which describes in detail the procedures followed in the library. [8]

Documenting the Procedures

A builder needs a blueprint. When I sew, I rely on a pattern and a list of instructions to guide me. Those who are expected to help with the cataloging process should have the procedures written out as well.

"The goal of every librarian is to get the material out on the shelves as soon as possible, for there they will be available for use," says Maryann J. Dotts. Hasty processing of materials often causes more problems than you wish to encounter. Take the time to follow your system of processing for all materials added to the library. [9] This is easier to do when procedures are available for frequent reference.

Record your policy decisions. Think through the entire process first. Then decide what is best. Record each step in enough detail so someone else can follow it. Even the rough draft will serve as a procedures manual.

Initially, your procedures may not be perfect. Expect some changes to be made as time goes by. However, for consistency, do not make a change unless it is clearly indicated after searching inspection. Then, be sure to record the change in your manual of instructions.

A case should be made for adopting and staying with standard library procedures. Libraries today have challenging opportunities to participate in cooperative activities. The use of standard cataloging enables them to merge files of information into a common catalog. For example, an interfaith group of librarians in Oil City, Pennsylvania, extended their outreach by creating such a catalog. They purchased a card catalog and received permission to place it in the public library. "The card catalog contains a file of their combined holdings, alphabetically arranged by author and title. Color-banded cards indicate which participating library has each book. Upon request at the circulation desk of the public library, the book is obtained for patrons for the customary two-week loan period."[10] Each participating library, of course, maintains its own catalog within the church or synagogue for use of its own congregation.

Gather together tools and aids for cataloging.

Outline "how to" for helpers. The CSLA guide on <u>Cataloging Books</u>

Step by Step was patterned after the procedures manual of one church library. The following is an example from it:

Step 16:   Cover the dust jacket with a plastic cover.

    a. Measure the height of the book in inches.

    b. Select a plastic cover that will fit. When in doubt choose the larger cover, as a crowded fit will wrinkle the paper jacket.

    c. Slip the paper jacket into the plastic cover and fit it around the book.

    d. Fasten the cover to the book.

        (1) Use permanent mending tape, or attaching tape.

        (2) Do not use cellophane tape. It will yellow, crack and peel off. [11]

Record all variations and exceptions to the general rule. For example: Use "Reference" above the call number for books to be added to the reference shelf; no card or pocket is needed.

Provide directions for users. Remember the users of the catalog as well. Consider directional cards in the catalog, signs posted nearby, or a leaflet of instructions introducing users to the library's content and arrangement (see Chapter 12).

Keep statistics. Count what you catalog. Designate a specific step along the way at which the count will be taken. This helps to insure accuracy. Some libraries merely count the work cards after the cataloging is completed.

Keep a running total of the number of items in the collection. Subtract items when they are withdrawn.

Statistics are very useful when you need to compile a report for the administrative board or other group of the congregation. They demonstrate how fast the collection is growing in numbers. They also indicate how actively the collection is being updated to remain current.

4/

Obtaining Supplies

"I've ordered some supplies," our education secretary greeted me as I walked in the door. Just the week before, books had been gathered from around the church to form the beginnings of a library.

"What did you order?" I asked in surprise.

"Oh, some cards and things," she replied and handed me a list. As an experienced librarian, I was almost afraid to look. The list read as follows:

1000 catalog cards	1 library paste
500 book cards	1 black engrossing ink
500 book pockets	1 white lettering ink
500 date due slips	1 dozen pen points
1 date stamp	6 book supports
1 ink pad	

"Francis told me what to order," she added, in response to my unspoken question. Francis was another librarian designated to help. I was pleased and relieved.

Locating Sources

Not everyone has the advice of a professional librarian when ordering cataloging supplies. Not every library will have exactly the same requirements. Quantities will depend largely on how many times you expect to catalog. The type of supplies you order will depend on the variety of media formats to be processed. Public and school librarians, because they are used to handling these materials and ordering supplies, can be a helpful source of advice.

Library-supply dealers. Begin by writing for catalogs from the library-supply dealers, such as:

Bro-Dart, Inc.

Eastern Division	Western Divison
1609 Memorial Avenue	1236 South Hatcher Street
Williamsport, PA 17701	City of Industry, CA 91749
Demco Educational Corp.	Western Regional Office:
Box 7488	Box 7767
Madison, WI 53707	Fresno, CA 93727

Gaylord Brothers, Inc.
Library Supplies & Equipment
Syracuse, NY 13201

Library Bureau (formerly Remington Rand Library Bureau)
Mohawk Valley Community Corp.
801 Park Avenue
Herkimer, NY 13350
(offices in principal cities)

Most public libraries will have the names and addresses of other dealers. Browse through these catalogs. Become familiar with quantities and quality of materials that are available.

Order supplies

Materials required for cataloging and preparing books for circulation might include the following:

Accession book record

Library name stamp

Catalog cards

Book cards

Book pockets

Date-due slips

Paste

Labels

Pen and lettering ink, or electric stylus and transfer paper

Guide cards for card catalog and shelf list file

Gift bookplates

Plastic jacket covers

Attaching tape and dispenser

Shellac

Denominational library services. Denominational bookstores and church library services sometimes offer library supplies as a part of their service. For example, Cokesbury (201 Eighth Avenue South, Nashville, TN 37202) has a Church Resource Library Starter Kit with basic materials to set up a church library. They have included in it 1 accession book, 2000 catalog cards, 500 plain book pockets, 500 book cards, 500 date due slips, 1 set catalog card guides (celluloid), 1 set shelf list guides, 1 adjustable dater, 1 stamp pad, 1 bone folder, 3 packages book plates, 1000 labels and 100 protectors.

The Christian Board of Publication (Box 179, St. Louis, MO 63166) offers a Library Supply Kit with 1 accession and financial record book, 100 book charging cards, 100 library card pockets, 500 library catalog cards, and 100 date-due slips.

There is no single answer to how many supplies you will need to begin and keep going. Based on your procedures, determine what supplies you need. The number of items cataloged each year will help you estimate future requirements.

Retail stores. Some of the materials used are standard office supplies: date stamp, ink pad, manila folders, etc. These usually can be purchased locally. The specialized library supplies, such as catalog cards, accession sheets, book pockets, etc., are seldom carried by retail stores. These must be ordered by mail from one of the above.

Cooperative arrangements. Cordial relationships with other libraries can pay off. At one time our church library was mending books sent to migrant workers on the eastern shore of Maryland. We ran out of repair materials. The public library loaned us enough to finish the job. As soon as our order came in, the materials were replaced.

Cooperative arrangements can help you take advantage of reduced prices for quantity sales. Investigate the possibility of pooling your orders with nearby libraries. The Church Library Council (in the greater Washington, D. C. area) ordered quantities of clear plastic Contac paper, in rolls, to cover paperback books. They arranged a mini-workshop to demonstrate the technique and allowed member libraries to buy the materials - at cost - until the supply was exhausted.

Record-Keeping Supplies

Regardless of the size of your collection, there is a need to keep track of items ordered, received and processed into the collection. Simple printed forms are available. They help one maintain these records. Such records identify property for inventory and insurance purposes. They are useful for budgeting and planning. For example, how many books did we add to the collection last year and at what cost? Good records promote good stewardship.

Order forms. When you order books and other materials, keep an order record in the library. This is useful to follow up on an order

59

if there is a long delay in receiving it.

Printed book-order forms are available from library-supply dealers. Generally, they are 3" x 5" in size and spaced for a typewriter. They come in white card stock or on lightweight paper for carbon-copy use. The original is sent to the dealer in place of a letter. The copy is kept as the library's record.

Multi-part order forms provide copies for other uses as well. Multi-copy forms with chemically treated paper (which eliminates the need for carbon paper) are offered by the Highsmith Co., Inc. (P. O. Box 25, Highway 106 East, Fort Atkinson, WI 53538). Their six-part form has the following copies:

original (white)	order copy for dealer
yellow	order LC cards
pink	library copy
green	work slip or fund copy
blue	library or dealer second copy
buff (ledger stock)	punched for temporary catalog card or shelf list

If used by the library, the blue copy can be used to send a follow-up inquiry. If sent to the dealer along with the original, it can be used by him to send a status report if the order is delayed.

An alternative to the printed order forms is a plain 3" x 5" file card. Record the author, title, publisher, price, etc., in the same way on each order. Be sure to include the date of the order and your own return address. Label it clearly as an "ORDER."

The advantage of producing a separate record for each item ordered is that it can be interfiled alphabetically by author or title in
a suspense file. As each item is received, that one record is removed
from the file and marked "received." Some libraries use this copy of
the order form as the work card for cataloging. If the information on
the form is not in the proper order for a catalog card, turn it over
and use the back. This one card then holds all the information you
need for accessioning, for the shelf list, and for identifying the
person who requested it.

Accession book. This is used to keep a numerical record of books
and other materials as they are added to the library. The first book
is number 1, the second is number 2, and so on. The accession number
gives each book a permanent identification number which can be used
in place of a copy number, if desired.

An accession book is a stiff-cover, three-ring binder that lies
flat when open. It holds loose-leaf printed sheets 9½" x 20" in size.
A small number of accession sheets come with the binder. Refill
sheets are purchased separately. The sheets come in pairs numbered
from 01 to (1)00. Each page has 25 entries. After the first 99 numbers are assigned, add the hundred number before the 00. Add the
same hundred number before the next sequence of 99 numbers.

An accession entry includes space for title, date of publication,
source, price and remarks.

Summary of additions and withdrawals. A similar loose-leaf record book is available to keep track of the monthly statistics for cataloging and for ciculation. The binders hold 8½" x 11" sheets. The sheets are imprinted with Dewey Decimal categories. The sheets headed "Reference" are used to record the number of items cataloged or withdrawn from the collection. The sheets headed "Circulation" keep track of material going out to users as circulation.

Periodical check-in cards. Since the "order" for a periodical subscription is received in installments all during the year, a special form is used to note receipt of issues. Preprinted cards are available for dailies, weeklies or monthlies. These usually are 3" x 5" in size. Across the top of the 5" side there is room to type the title, number of copies and the expiration date. There are little boxes to check when an issue is received.

The daily or weekly check-in card has the months listed down from the top and the dates (1 through 31) across the top. The monthly check-in card has the years listed down from the top and the months (January through December) across the top.

The periodical check-in card tells you at a glance whether or not an expected issue has come. It also tells you when you need to renew the subscription.

Book circulation records. Printed circulation statistics forms keep track of daily, monthly and yearly records of books that go out into circulation. Whether or not they are kept on a printed form, these records should be kept.

A-V record cards. Media materials other than books are tricky to keep track of because of their variety in format, handling and use. Library-supply catalogs often devote an entire section to these special materials. Record-keeping devices range from magnetic/markable control-board kits to simple record cards. These may be used for scheduling as well as circulating filmstrips, disc records, slides, etc.

Supplies for Cataloging and Processing

Right from the beginning you will need supplies for cataloging and preparing materials for use.

Identification stamp. A library name stamp is a "must" and one item that we almost forgot when we first started assembling our cataloging materials. A rubber stamp with the name and location of the library can be ordered from any stationery store. It may be as large or as small as you like. Examples:

United Church Library
Bethesda, Maryland

or

Memorial Library
Bethesda United Church
Bethesda, MD

Some libraries prefer an embossing stamp which presses through the paper and makes an inkless impression like a corporation seal.

Others prefer to use bookplates, which also serve to identify gifts and memorials.

Gift bookplates encourage the giving of books to the library. They are available from the denominational publishing houses with inscriptions: "Presented by...," "In Honor of...," or "In Memory of...." Paste bookplates inside the front cover. If plastic jacket covers obscure that area, paste them on the page facing the inside of the cover. If there are elaborate maps or other printing on the end papers, turn to the first all-white page or use the page that faces the title page.

Catalog cards are used to make a card index of materials in the library. They are approximately 3" x 5" in size (exactly 7.5 x 12.5 cm., per Bureau of Standards pattern) and have a hole punched in the center bottom for a round rod to hold the cards in a drawer.

Catalog cards are available in three weights - light, medium and heavy. Heavy weight stands up best under constant use and is most expensive. Many libraries use the medium or light weight and find them quite satisfactory. The Library of Congress prints its catalog cards on medium weight. When you always buy the same weight cards, you are sure to have a more uniform catalog.

Cards can be furnished plain (unlined) or with rulings, as illustrated in the supply catalogs. Most libraries use plain cards. Plain cards look neater in the file. Typewriter spacing maintains the even margins and indentions. However, cards with printed lines are available, generally as follows:

One vertical red line at left margin (first indention).

One horizontal red line across the top and two vertical
   red lines - at first and second indentions.

Same as above, with additional horizontal lines in blue
   throughout the card.

Color-coded cards identify non-book materials, such as films,
tapes, etc. These come in a variety of colors - either a solid-color
card or a white card with a 3/16" color band across the top on both
sides of the card. Color-coded cards seldom are lined.

  Book cards are charging cards. They keep a record of who has
borrowed the book. One is required for each book cataloged. They are
3" x 5" in size and upright. At the top of the 3" side there is space
for the call number, accession number (and/or copy number), author and
title. The remainder of the card is ruled - both sides - to provide
space for the borrower's name and, usually, the date borrowed. Some
cards leave space to record the date returned.

  Book cards are light and medium weight. They come in color, if
desired. If no preference is given, suppliers will send lightweight
white, which is most commonly used.

  Book pockets are designed to hold the book card in each book.
They are strong enough to withstand wear and tear and light enough to
be used in a typewriter.

  Book pockets come in various styles, light and medium weight, and
usually are manila color. They can be ordered with the library name

and location printed on them, or the library name and rules for bor-rowing books. Needless to say, printing costs money, and the plain pockets are cheaper. One book pocket is needed for each book.

Date slips are white, usually 3" x 5" in size, and often gummed along the back of the top edge. They are ruled for date due or date loaned. One slip is required for each book.

A combined pocket and date slip also is available. Rulings for date due or loaned are printed right on the pocket.

Paste is used for pasting the pockets in the books. A good paste will stick quickly without drying too fast. It will stay sweet and not get hard or lumpy. Standard library paste fills this description. It also can be thinned with water. A pint will last quite a long time.

Date stamp and pad. Get a date stamp that is small enough to fit into small columns, but large enough to be read easily. A date stamp with adjustable date bands is recommended. Use the date stamp for ordering, accessioning, cataloging and circulating materials. Be sure to get a stamp pad to go with it.

Labels are used for inscribing call numbers or other identifica-tion marks on the outside of books and other materials. They come in a variety of sizes and materials. Select for permanence, but remember you might want to remove one on occasion to correct an error or change a classification. Select sizes and shapes suitable for your purposes and always buy the same - for a consistent and neat labeling job.

For most uses, pressure-sensitive labels which are self-adhesive are recommended. The standard plastic-impregnated ones work well for backs of books, metal reels, cardboard containers, etc. They are moisture-resistant. They also are cheaper than the super-stick or the cloth (fabric).

Super-stick pressure-sensitive labels are quite permanent. They will adhere even to old pebbled-cloth book covers. But they are difficult to remove.

Cloth (fabric) pressure-sensitive labels are best. They adhere to textured or uneven surfaces and are most adaptable in conforming to contours. They are the most durable and the most expensive. They also are considerably superior to the paste-on cloth labels, which tend to peel and come off rough bindings.

Labels can be reinforced or protected in one of the following ways:
Use see-through label protectors, available from the library-
    supply dealers.
Brush or spray on clear plastic, made especially for books.
Affix a strip of permanent mending tape across the label.
Drop a daub of liquid plastic (Elmer's glue) on the label
    and spread it over the edges and onto the book with a
    finger. The glue will be clear when dry.

A small hand-held labeling machine is available which embosses letters or numbers on plastic adhesive-backed tape and cuts the tape to any length desired. These machines are available at most stationery stores and library-supply dealers. Some make larger size letters than others. The length of the call number determines the length of the label. The tape is available in a variety of colors. The machine requires no special skills and anyone can operate it quite easily.

Another alternative method of labeling books is to hand letter directly on the spines. Some librarians prefer this because it is cheaper and the lettering is not confined to the space of a paste-on label. It can be adjusted according to need. When printing obscures the field where the call number is to be lettered, simply draw a plain black label on the binding with pen and permanent black ink. Then use white ink to letter the number. An electric lettering pencil and transfer paper also can be used instead of the pen and ink.

Pen and ink. The choice of either a bowl or stub point pen is a matter of preference. Choose one that will help you produce bold and neat lettering. Use a permanent lettering ink, which comes in black, white or gold.

Electric pencil and transfer paper. An electric pencil - much like the stylus in a child's woodburning set - heats to transfer hand lettering from coated paper to the backs of books. It comes with a cork protector in the handle, an on-and-off switch and about five feet of rubber-covered cord. The pencil is used in any standard outlet and has two interchangeable writing points that easily unscrew from the handle when the pencil is not in use. One is for standard lettering with medium lines. The other is for fine lines and letters. There is no spill or running of ink and no waiting to dry.

Transfer paper comes in colors such as black, white, blue, orange, silver and gold. It is about 7/8" wide and comes packed in small round containers like typewriter ribbons. The paper is cut or torn off the roll as it is used.

Jacket covers. Transparent plastic book-jacket covers protect the dust jackets that come on new books. Plastic-covered jackets keep your books looking bright and new. They not only protect the bindings from wear but stimulate circulation by colorfully displaying the book. The dust jacket often is more attractive than the book itself. Our public librarian once said that when two copies of the same book are side by side on the shelf, the one with the plastic cover will always go out first. The plastic jacket covers are one way to preserve the sales appeal of the book.

Book-jacket covers come in standard book sizes. They also come in rolls, adjustable to a variety of book sizes. We started out using the individual covers and found we frequently ran out of a needed size, while we had others on hand an unusually long time. We switched to the adjustable covers in rolls and found them to be quite practical. Care needs to be used in applying them to keep them neat and smooth.

Guide cards are used in all card files. Alphabetical guides as well as plain guides are available from the library-supply dealers with holes punched for the rods. Plain guide cards with half- or third-cut tabs are meant to be hand-lettered or typed. The half-cut tabs provide a tab that runs half way across the card. The cards alternate so the tab appears on the left on one card and the right of the next.

Third-cut tabs provide a tab that runs one-third of the way across the card. The first tab is at the left, the next card tab is in the center, and the third is at the right. We use the half-cut tab plain guides as well as the alphabet guides in the card catalog, as follows:

C

CHILDREN

CHRISTIAN LIFE

CHRISTIANITY

CHRISTMAS

CHURCH HISTORY

CLERGY

Plastic protectors are an alternative guide. They slip over a standard card and hold it ½" above the other cards to serve as a guide. These are hole punched and come in clear as well as colored plastic. Some are merely color-banded, with a 1/8" color band across the top of a clear protector.

Card-catalog cabinet. Before you invest in equipment to hold cards, look ahead. Never buy major equipment until you have had time to study the goals of your library and plan the overall operation. Some questions you need to answer are: How many books and other materials do you expect eventually to have? How big should the catalog be to hold the cards for your maximum collection? Do you have the room and/or the funds for it now? If not, consider equipment that can expand and grow with the collection. Do you want metal or wood? What other furnishings will be in the library? What colors are in your scheme of decoration?

We managed to get along with a cardboard box for our card catalog until we were ready to plan a library room and the furnishings to equip it. Christine Buder says: "Many libraries start their catalogs in inexpensive cardboard boxes, but usually find it necessary to replace them with cabinets of somewhat sturdier construction." She recommends a well-built wood or metal card catalog case with at least two drawers.[1] Max Celnik advises: "Free-standing cases are more satisfactory than built-ins. Cases may be bought in four to sixty tray units, and new units may be added as needed. Even a small library should begin with a nine-tray case."[2] On the other hand, our own church library now has a fifteen-drawer wooden cabinet. Three drawers hold the shelf list. This is not at all too large for the collection of 4,000 books and other media materials.

Supplies for Circulation and Storage

When books and other materials are cataloged and ready for shelf display, you will need book supports, a charging tray (with guides), shelf markers , and possibly display racks. These come in different finishes and colors. Will you want gray, black or green? Wood or metal? Without a plan for the future this can be a hard decision to make - especially if your library is a temporary section of unfinished shelving and no promise of a good location in view. Nevertheless, you must think in terms of ideals - of dreams and color schemes - before you order. Buy even the few things you need as though your dream library were a reality. This helps to achieve the dream while you are waiting for it.

Book supports to hold books erect on the shelf are a must. They need not be fancy. I knew a library that in its early stages created a bright and colorful effect inexpensively by covering bricks with cloth. Any number of satisfactory "make-due" book supports can be devised to serve the purpose until you are ready to buy the real thing.

Bookends are available, usually metal, either plain or with cork or felt bottoms. The plain bottoms slide along the shelf and slip under the books easily. The cork or felt bottoms hold their place on the shelf better.

Rubber-tipped book poles can be used in place of bookends. Spring tension holds them in place like a lamp pole. This provides an answer for those large picture books.[3]

Charging tray. You will need something to hold the cards for material in circulation - the circulation file. We used a 3" X 5" file box until we were able to get a library desk. The top right-hand drawer of the desk is designed (deep enough) to be used as a charging tray. Charging trays 5" high and 3" wide are available separately. They can be placed on top of a desk or table.

Pamphlet boxes and shelf files for magazines, newspapers and other hard-to-file items are available in a variety of styles, materials and colors. They range from cardboard fold-outs with open tops and diagonal cuts to metal "Princeton" files with open tops and backs and a metal strip across the front for maximum visibility of material filed. The sturdiest boxes are the most expensive. All can be filed on the shelf along with books.

Try making an inexpensive pamphlet box from an empty soap box (make sure it is clean). Cut off the top. Make a diagonal cut from the top of one narrow side to halfway down the other. Cover the box with Contac paper.

Pamphlet binders come in various sizes and styles, which are described fully in the supply catalogs. The simplest is two covers joined by a gummed binding strip which can be moistened on the outside to fasten a pamphlet permanently into the cover. These come in sizes ranging from 7" X 5" to 14" X 11". We found that the 9" X 7" size would handle most pamphlets and helped to make varying sizes look uniform on the shelf.

Media files are used to file audio-visual materials on the shelf and to protect them while in circulation. They come in a wide variety of sizes and in single- or mixed-media styles. In these boxes, A-Vs can be stacked horizontally or filed upright alongside books. Usually, they are corrugated fiberboard or corrugated plastic. Suppliers quite often will send free samples on request.

Supplies for Mending and Repair

Even when a library is new, there will be some books that need mending before they are cataloged. For example, you receive as a gift a very useful book that is slightly damaged, or a child borrows a book and baby brother tears a page. Be prepared to mend and repair. Know how to do it and what supplies will be needed.

"Mending kits" are available from library-supply dealers. However, these sometimes contain supplies not really essential for a basic kit.

73

Most minor book problems can be repaired with the following:

Permanent mending tape and dispenser

Plastic concentrate adhesive, or library paste

Long-handled paste brush, or thin stick

Perforated adhesive cloth

Mystic tape in various widths

Scissors

Rubber eraser

Permanent mending tape is used for repairing those torn pages.
Never use Scotch cellophane tape for this purpose, as the edges gum
and with age it turns yellow and brittle. When it finally falls off
it leaves an unsightly mark where it was attached. Permanent mending
tape is opaque, never gums at the edges, and keeps its color. It comes
in ½" and 3/4" widths and is self-adhering. We use the ½" because it
is cheaper and seems to do an adequate job.

Plastic concentrate adhesive is used by some libraries. Regular
library paste is preferred by others. The plastic is a stronger adhesive and dries quickly. Either may be used for replacing torn-out
pages. Just put a very thin line of it along the torn edge of the
loose page, insert the page in place, and close the book. A light
hand is needed, so that excess paste or plastic does not ooze where
it is not wanted. Too much adhesive can foul up the job.

Perforated adhesive cloth is a strong white cloth strip, gummed
on one side and perforated down the center. The 1" width generally is
used, but it also comes in 3/4". This forms a hinge - the perforation

at the hinge - between the first sheet or end paper of the book and the rest of the pages. Books start to come apart here. Perforated adhesive cloth reinforces the hinge. If the cover and end paper have pulled away completely from the main body of the book, it is wise to consider rebinding. Before rebinding, however, make sure the book is really worth keeping and that rebinding is cheaper than buying a new copy.

Mystic tape covers worn spines. It comes in widths of 3/8", 3/4", 1½", 2", 3" and 4" and in many colors, including white, red, blue, black, brown, maroon and green. Black is quite commonly used for this purpose because it tends to obscure the wrinkles. Narrower sizes can be used to reinforce pamphlets, thin picture books or magazines. (Opaque reinforcing tape also does a good job of reinforcing paper covers and has the added advantage of transparency.)

When you recover a spine with Mystic tape, cut it at least ½" longer at the top and at the bottom than the size of the book. Slit the excess length at the hinge, both top and bottom, where both covers meet the spine. Fold down the tabs thus formed inside the covers. Trim with a scissors the excess that remains above and below the spine itself, or fold it over on itself to form a point (like a paper hat) and tuck it in between the spine and the spine binding.

Rubber eraser or artgum eraser takes off pencil marks and other smudges from pages. Book cleaner is used to freshen soiled bindings made of cloth or leather. Likewise, some furniture polishes (the ones which say they will) are used to remove mildew from cloth or leather bindings. In damp basements (and what church doesn't have them?) this can be a useful thing to know.

Repair booklets. Library-supply dealers sometimes offer booklets
on how to mend and repair books. These generally give detailed instructions, with illustrations. Two such are Demco Library Supplies
and Gaylord Brothers, Inc.

Estimating Requirements

Deciding which supplies to buy is much like making out a shopping
list for groceries. Consider the job to be done, how much time you
have to do it, and what materials you already have on hand. What do
you need to get?

Selecting supplies. Review your cataloging procedures step by
step. What supplies are required? Use the earlier part of this chapter as a checklist. Study the supply catalogs, too. Keep a record of
choices so you can reorder the same thing next time.

Figure five catalog cards per book - for the card catalog and the
shelf list - and one book card, pocket and label for each book. The
other media items will need catalog cards and labels, too. Remember
the paste (for the pockets). Are you well equipped to letter the labels? Add other items that will make the job easier or more complete:
date slips, bookplates, jacket covers, etc.

How many of each? Prices are cheaper if you order a larger quantity. Yet you will not want to order more than you need or can afford
to buy at any one time.

Projecting annual needs. Look back over the previous years' statistics. How many volumes were added each year? What was the size of your budget? These figures will give you some idea of what to expect in the coming year, unless there are drastic changes in the operation. Statistics of previous years will help you estimate the number of gifts you are likely to receive, how many of the needed resources you probably can afford to purchase, and how much time you have to catalog and prepare materials for use (do not purchase more than you can reasonably handle).

Example

	Past Year	Coming Year
Books		
Gifts	27	30
Purchases	360	400
Total	387	430
Periodicals	4	5
Other Media Materials		
Filmstrips	10	10
Cassettes	17	25
Games	2	5
Kits	3	5
Other	0	5
Total	38	50
Total Resources	429	485

What supplies do you already have on hand to catalog the anticipated resource materials? Look at the cost of materials. Can you afford to buy enough to last the year? If not, how much can you spend now? When you calculate how much or how many supplies you need, allow a certain amount for inadvertent processing errors.

Example:

Supplies Needed	Cost $/500 or	On Hand	Purchase
2400 catalog cards	$/1000	600	1000
430 book cards	$/500	30	500
430 book-pocket/due slips	$/500	100	500
430 book labels	$/1000	300	1000
10 filmstrip labels	$/roll	½ roll	none
25 cassette labels	$/roll	none	1 roll
25 cassette-box labels	$/roll	none	1 roll
15 general A-V labels	$/roll	3/4 roll	none
5 periodical check-in	$/500	490	none

A careful projection of your shopping needs for the coming year will help in preparing a budget. It also will help to get the best buy in supplies without overloading the closet.

5/

Preparing to Catalog

"Requests have been made to me from persons rejuvenating old libraries," writes Rachel Kohl, chairman of the Library Services Committee of the Church and Synagogue Library Association. "Their main concern seems to be what to do with an existing collection, how to catalog such a collection, especially if it has been partially done before." [1]

This made me think of a favorite game my son once had. When you would reach a certain step on the path toward "Goal" it would tell you to "go back to Start." This usually was accompanied by a groan from the player as he realized that, after effort, he was going to have to begin all over again. This is good advice for librarians, too. Every once in a while it is good to stop and review what you are doing and why. Go back to the beginning again.

Existing collections should be in a continuous process of rejuvenation. If they are not, they soon become stagnant and die. Evaluate an older collection as though you were starting anew. Review the previous chapters. Restate your aims. Look at the general arrangement of materials. Establish policies and guidelines based on present goals (which might be quite different from previous ones). Screen the collection and discard resource materials which are no longer wanted (old-looking or worn out) and no longer needed (outdated for current programs and concerns). Then, proceed as though the remaining collection were a new gift. Review (and correct if necessary) the cataloging of each item to be consistent with current guidelines.

Screening Materials

Whether a library is well established, being revitalized or just beginning, the material coming in needs to be screened.

Gifts are likely to come in first. Some probably will be relatively new (perhaps book-club selections). Others will be well used - favorites from a deceased minister's library, books found in an attic or basement during clean-up, or children's books and records that have been outgrown (some in need of repair). Be sure to advise donors that if the gifts cannot be used in the library they will be passed along to another library or to someone else who can use them.

Review the policy you established for selecting materials. It will be your ultimate guide in screening and a justification for refusing a gift or for taking an item out of the collection. Duplicate copies of good material can be shared with church libraries - perhaps those in less advantaged areas of the neighborhood. We contribute withdrawn items to the annual used-book sale sponsored by the young people of the church. An active, current library must be reviewed and weeded continuously to keep it that way.

Purchases. Orders will be placed for the purchase of resources. (Make sure these fit your selection policy, too.) When materials come in, make sure you receive what you ordered.

Pull the copy of your outstanding order. Check the dealer's invoice against the shipment to make sure that each item listed is actually in the box. Notify the dealer as soon as possible if there are missing items, wrong titles, errors in pricing or damaged contents. If materials must be returned, take care that they are sent so they will arrive back at the dealer in the same condition you received them. If the shipment checks out, take your copy of the order, mark it "received" with the date, and slip it inside the front cover of the book or fasten it (if possible) to other media.

Open each new book properly.

Opening the new book. A new book must be opened properly the first time it is opened, so the spine will not crack:

Hold the book upright, with the spine on a flat surface.

Open both covers, holding the pages together in the upright
position. Press your fingers along the inside fold, between the covers and the rest of the book.

Take a small section of pages from each side and open them
against the covers. Press your fingers along the inside
fold.

Repeat the above until you reach the center of the book.

Go through the book page by page. Look for misprints or
missing pages. (Return faulty copies for replacement.)
Cut any uncut pages with a letter opener.

Judging permanence. Consider whether the book has temporary or permanent value to the collection. Does it need to be cataloged as a book or will it serve better in the pamphlet file? Does it need to be cataloged at all? For example, when multiple copies of a study book are received, you might not want to catalog them all. One copy might be classified and added to the collection and the others just distributed as needed. Another example is very inexpensive children's picture books. You might wish to put these in the pre-school classroom with no strings attached (not cataloged or circulated as a part of the library collection).

Clean and repair. Does the book need mending? It should be in good condition for circulation before it is placed on the shelf. Have

the proper mending supplies handy. Repair those torn pages or frayed
edges. If a picture book has lost its cover, try making one, as follows:

Materials:

2 pieces of cardboard

1 roll Contac paper or plastic-coated shelf liner

1 roll Mystic tape and 2 strips of perforated adhesive cloth

1 picture

Directions:

Cut two pieces of cardboard slightly larger than the size
of the pages.

Cover the cardboard with Contac paper or plastic-coated shelf
liner.

Cut a piece of Mystic tape two inches longer than the cardboard. Center the two pieces of cardboard on the sticky
side of the tape so that there is the width of the book
spine between them and one inch of tape extending to the
top and bottom.

Fold the tape extension down onto the covered cardboard.

Center the book spine on the sticky part of the Mystic tape
between the covers.

Cut two strips of perforated adhesive cloth the length of
the cover. Paste each between the book and the cover, to
form a hinge. This fastens the cover securely to the
book.

Cut a color picture from a greeting card or magazine and

paste it on the front cover. If desired, letter the
title at the top.

Book cleaner brightens up a soiled cloth binding. A gum eraser
does wonders on pencil marks and smudges. Plastic spray, while still
wet, will help to wipe off a mistake made with the stylus and transfer
paper. Plastic spray also brightens up and protects an entire binding
after the book is properly lettered. This is especially good for children's books.

High humidity and temperature often make mildew and mold on books
a real problem. There are preparations available that claim to take
care of this, including some furniture polishes. However, the following formula was tested at the Duke Hospital Library and found to be
successful as a preventative as well as a remedy:

   10 grams of thymol crystals

    4 grams of mercuric bichloride

   200 cc. of ether

   400 cc. of benzene

Apply it with a sponge or small dishmop. It dries almost immediately
without leaving a precipitate or changing the color of the binding.
The odor disappears quickly. Be careful, though. The solution is
highly inflammable and must be kept away from fire. To protect the
hands while doing the work, hold the pages of the book without touch-
ing the binding. This also works for other leather products, such as
albums and luggage. [2]

If most of your books are not bright and new, make them look as attractive as possible.

Accessioning

The accession record is a listing of the books and other materials in the library in the order of their receipt. Each volume received is entered on a separate line that is numbered consecutively, like the checks in a checkbook. Space is provided for author, title, date, source, price and remarks.

Why. The accession book is kept as a permanent record for property identification. Its advantages are many, as follows. It provides in one place a record of all additions - purchases as well as gifts - and indicates when they are added and withdrawn from the collection. It assigns a unique property number that is never used again for any other item in the collection - therefore, it can be used in place of a copy number. It tells at a glance how many books and other items are in the collection (by keeping a running total of items as they are withdrawn, you can subtract this number from the highest number assigned to determine the collection's size). It serves as a required record for insurance purposes (record the cost of purchase and the estimated value of gifts as you go along; then, add up the columns to determine the value of the collection). Finally, it keeps other statistics, such as how many books were purchased during the year, how many gifts were received (and from whom), which funds were used, etc. - This information is useful for making annual reports.

Large libraries often give up keeping an accession book when the volume of material they handle makes it impractical. Instead, they record business information (date received, source and price) on the shelf-list card and keep statistics in other ways.

An accession record is recommended for church and synagogue libraries. It is a reassuring anchor and a permanent record of growth. This is especially important if you are new at the job or there is a rapid turnover of volunteer help on the staff.

How. The accession book's loose-leaf sheets are printed with numbers from 01 through 99. Record each volume on a separate line. This assigns the number on that line to that book. After you have entered 99 books, add a number 1 before the 00 at the end of the page. Type or write the number 1 before all the numbers on the next set of sheets that go from 01 to 99, for 100. Next add a 2 for 200, and so on.

Write or type the current date to the left and above the next number assigned each day when you sit down to accession a pile of books. Assign each number in order by filling in the information for each volume: author (last name generally is enough), title (sub-titles are not necessary), publisher (short form of name or abbreviation), year of publication and cost (or estimated value of gift). Under remarks note the fund name or number, or the donor's name.

When a number is assigned, write it on the order slip for that book or on a 3" x 5" slip or card that will be used as the work card for cataloging.

When a book is withdrawn from the library, draw a line through its entry in the accession book, writing or stamping the word "withdrawn" with the date. A small rubber stamp that says "withdrawn" keeps the record book looking neat.

Each book in the library - including duplicate copies or volumes in a set - is assigned an accession number of its own. If a lost book is replaced, the new copy is given a new accession number. A number, once assigned, is never used again.

All types of media in the collection are accessioned. However, many libraries prefer to maintain separate books or separate sections within one book for the various types. Each type is identified by alphabetical letters or an abbreviation which precedes the accession number (for example, "FS-1" for filmstrips). Each media series begins with the number 1.

Periodical issues. Individual issues of current periodical subscriptions are not accessioned. They are recorded on a periodical check-in card.

Make sure each issue is received. If one does not arrive, send a "claim" notice to the subscription source. Let them know you did not get it. A replacement will be sent to you.

When periodical issues are accumulated and bound into a single volume, the volume is accessioned - either as a book or as a media series with its own set of accession numbers.

Memorial albums. Many church and synagogue libraries like to maintain a separate record of all gifts and memorials - furniture, draperies and carpeting, as well as books and other resource materials that have been given as gifts. This is an additional record kept for a completely different purpose other than cataloging.

Denominational supply catalogs generally list "In Remembrance" books which are used for this purpose. They generally are handsome, loose-leaf albums with red cover embossed in gold. Album pages are printed with spaces for the names of donors, the gift presented, and the person in whose memory (or honor) it was given.

Memorial albums are nice to display from time to time - perhaps with some of the memorial gifts. Memorial Day weekend provides an excellent opportunity to tie in with a current holiday and call attention to the fact that the library appreciates receiving gifts.

Marking Material

Ownership is marked by stamping the library's name and location somewhere on the item. In a book, the ownership stamp generally is placed on the title page, and perhaps on the "secret" page or edges of pages. Some libraries also use bookplates inside the front cover.

Write the accession number in ink either in or on the item itself. In a book, this usually is written on the right-hand page following the title page, but individual library practices vary. Some libraries prefer to record all the information about a book on the title page itself. Always write it in the same place in each book.

The accession number for media materials other than books quite

often is used as the call number. Make sure it is on a label that
is clearly visible.

Assembling Tools

Make sure the tools you need are readily available nearby. These
include the following:

Library's procedures manual

Classification guide

Subject heading list

Card catalog

Shelf-list file

Now you are ready to catalog.

6/

Cataloging Books

We sat around in an informal circle, meeting as the working library staff. The new church season would soon begin and we wanted to be prepared. Resources were coming in for the fall teaching curriculum and already the teachers were inquiring for the materials. We were trying to get organized to make the best use of the time we had available to catalog and process the materials for use.

"After Marge makes out the work card and checks the catalog, I can assign the classification numbers and subject headings. Then, who will type the cards? Yes, you can take them home to do. All the information you need will be on the work card. All right, Marie will do the typing. Stewart, would you be willing to help out with the labeling? That would be great. What would you think of asking the Scouts who are working on God and Country Awards to help with the pasting of pockets and affixing of jacket covers. That's a good idea. Mildred, would you be willing to coordinate that with Dr. C.?"

So it went. A big job divided into enough parts soon becomes a smaller one. When all tasks were assigned we were ready to begin.

Making the Work Card

Begin with the work card. This is the rough draft of information needed for typing cards and getting the book ready for use. In getting ready to catalog, you recorded the accession number on a 3" x 5" slip of paper or card or on the back of the order slip. That is a beginning. Next, add other elements of information in the same general format as the typed card. The following is a typical work card:

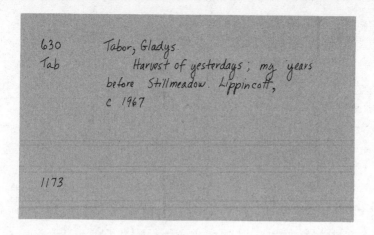

630
Tab
    Tabor, Gladys.
        Harvest of yesterdays; my years
    before Stillmeadow. Lippincott,
    c 1967

1173

Elements of information. In simplified cataloging, the basic catalog-card information consists of author, title, publisher, and date - in that order. Some books have an illustrator, compiler, editor or translator. If so, and this information is important enough to record, add it after the title. Insert next the edition (if not the first). Then record the publisher and date. Following this information, note the number of volumes (if more than one).

Most of the basic cataloging information is found on the title page. This is the page near the front of a book that identifies the author, title and publisher. The title page is the authority for cataloging information.

If notes are desired, such as age group, contents, etc., they are added farther down on the work card, but above the accession number.

Main entry. The first item of information to fill in on the work card is the name of the person or group responsible for the intellectual content of the book. Usually, this is a person as author. This is the author card and will be filed by author in the catalog. It is called the main entry card because all other cards that are made are exact duplicates of it, with a line of information inserted at the top for filing purposes.

Author names. If a person authored the book, copy his/her name from the title page, last name first. Omit titles such as "Dr." and "Mrs." If there is more than one author, use the name of the first one as the main entry. (The names of all the authors will be identified later.)

The name to be used for saints, popes and nuns can be a problem, according to Betty Lou Hammargren. She cites an example, The Story of a Soul; Autobiography by St. Therese of Lisieux, translated by Clark (Westminster, MD, Christian Classics, 1975). Should the author card be under her family name, Martin? Or, should Clark, the translator, be shown as the author? In practice, saints are entered as follows: Therese of Lisieux, Saint. The entry for a pope would be: John XXIII, Pope. The entry for a nun would use the family name: Jones, Mary Ellen, Sister.[1]

Names that begin with a prefix such as "de" or "la," usually are entered under the prefix, as follows: Ten Boom, Corrie. Check aids

such as Akers Simple Library Cataloging, revised and rewritten by

Arthur Curley and Jana Varlejs (Metuchen, NJ, Scarecrow Press, 1977)

for how to record other unusual author names.

Sacred books do not have a person as author, so the main entry

is as follows: "Bible. Old Testament. Psalms."

An institution as author, rather than an individual, is entered

as follows: The United Methodist Church.

For government publications, the main entry is as follows: U.S.

Department of Agriculture.

See the sample cards for other examples of main entries.

Titles. Copy the title from the title page, on the line below

the author. Capitalize the first word of the title and proper names

only.

Sub-titles may be used or not. Use the sub-title if it will pro-

vide useful information for a potential reader. Place a semi-colon

after the title (unless the title ends with a question or exclamation

mark) and add the sub-title. End with a period.

A title printed on the cover or the dust jacket might be different

from the title on the title page. Ask yourself: Will someone be apt

to ask for this book by that title? If so, copy it mid-way down on

the card, as follows: "Cover title: Good news for modern man." It will be picked up as a note on the catalog card. (Notes are explained later.)

A popular title - a way of referring to the book that is not really its title - also can be picked up in a note, as follows: "Popular title: Modern version of the Bible."

<u>Joint authors, editors, etc</u>. If a book has more than one author, only the first one will have been picked up as the main entry. Therefore, identify both (or all) of the authors directly after the title. For example: "..., by Maud and Miska Petersham." If the book has a translator, editor, compiler, illustrator, etc., enter these next, as follows:

Trans. by ...

Ed. by ...

Comp. by ...

Illus. by ...

<u>Edition</u>. Copy the revision or edition next - <u>if</u> it appears on the title page. One assumes that a book is in its original edition unless the title page clearly states that it is a revised edition.

Minor changes or corrections sometimes are made when a book is reprinted but this alone does not make it a revised edition. A paperback edition, for example, might be a reprint of the original book with a different publisher's name (and possibly date). This can be treated as an added copy by adding a note to the catalog cards, as follows: "Paperback edition published by Bantam, 1977."

When the title page indicates that the book is a revised edition, the book is cataloged as a new title. It will have its own unique call number and its own set of catalog cards.

Frequently, revisions are issued in numbered editions and the title stays the same. These may be cataloged as an "open entry." Leave a blank space on the work card for the date of publication and add a note midway down on the card, to show what the library has. Example:

Library has

9th ed. 1972
10th ed. 1976

This holding information is added to the main entry card only. A directional note may be added to the other cards in the set. Example: "(See main entry card for library holdings.)" The accession number for each volume will be added to the shelf-list card. Example:

#467   9th ed. 1972
#1052 10th ed. 1976

To identify the shelf location of each, add the date below the call number - on the label, book card and pocket. Example:

016   016
Aud   Aud
1972   1976

Imprint. The next item of information to be copied onto the work card is the imprint - the publisher and date of publication. Write the publisher's name in brief. Example: "Revell" for "The Fleming H. Revell Company." After a comma, copy the date of publication. Example:

"Revell, c1976."

For date of publication use the copyright date, rather than a date from the title page. The copyright date usually is printed on the back of the title page. If the book has more than one copyright date, use the most recent one. If there is no copyright date at all, use any other date for the book that you can find. Examples:

c1977   (copyright date)

p1977   (preface date)

1977   (title page date)

(1977) (date found in a reference)

n.d.   (no date)

Translate Roman numerals into Arabic numerals. Look up the meaning of the Roman numerals in the appendix of an unabridged dictionary, or call the reference desk of your local public library for help.

Volumes. Sometimes a book will be published in more than one volume. It still requires only one set of catalog cards. After the above information, record the total number of volumes (if more than one) on the work card. Example "3v." Be sure the accession number for each volume is on the work card. This will be copied onto the shelf-list card when it is typed. Example:

#1135 v.1
#1136 v.2
#1137 v.3

To identify the shelf location of each volume, add the volume number below the call number - on the label, book card and pocket.

96

Example:

```
226     226     226
And     And     And
v.1     v.2     v.3
```

Notes. Explanatory notes quite often are useful on the catalog card. These might be contents, summary, age group, series, formerly published as, cover title, etc. (See sample cards.)

Annotations. When you have the book in hand, write a brief description of the book on the work card. Brief annotations can be used as summary notes on the catalog cards, an enrichment of the list of new additions you will type when the cataloging is completed, or a reminder for selecting additional subject headings.

This completes the information copied from the book itself.

Classifying a Book

Check the card catalog to see if the book has been cataloged already. If so, this is an added copy - a duplicate. Write the call number on the work card in the upper left corner and mark the card "added copy." This will be a flag to you to pull the shelf-list card from the file and add the accession number of the duplicate copy. If the book has not been cataloged, it is a new addition. It will need to be classified.

Before you grab your Dewey, Jacqulyn Anderson advises, take time to study the book. The primary step is to determine the subject. From then on, classification is really a mechanical process. Many persons fly by this vital first step.[2]

The first step is to determine what the book is all about. What is the subject, really? Look for the clues.

Title and sub-title. The title itself often tells you all you need to know about the subject of a book. For example: Easy Bulletin Boards by Melvyn K. Bowers. Sometimes it is the sub-title that is specific enough to help identify the subject. Example: Armed With Love; Stories of the Disciples by Gerald N. Battle. Then, some titles just do not tell enough and more information is needed. Example: The Irrational Season by Madeleine L'Engle.

Jacket blurb. On the inside flap of the paper dust jacket on a new book, there often appears a brief description of the book. This is called the jacket blurb. It is intended to help sell the book and, in most cases, it pinpoints the subject quite well. So read the jacket blurb, if the book has one.

Table of contents. Sometimes the titles of the chapters identify the book's contents quite well. On the contents page there quite often is additional information under each chapter heading. Look over the table of contents.

Introduction or preface. Especially if written by the author, an introduction or preface will explain the scope and limitations of the book. However, not all books contain one.

Index. A non-fiction book is likely to have an index in the back. This is an excellent clue to the content.

This helps to decide which number is best for your purposes. When
you have chosen the number, write it in the upper left corner of the
work card.

Special problems. If the book includes more than one major subject, which subject will determine its classification? An example
is Psychology and Christianity; the View Both Ways by Malcolm A. Jeeves.
The rule of thumb is: if one subject appears to have been treated more
fully, classify the book there. If both subjects appear to have been
treated equally, decide in which place the book will be most useful in
your library and classify it there.

Occasionally a book with only one major subject could be classed
in more than one place. An example is Plants of the Bible. There is
a number for Ancient Plants (581.93) which comes under the hierarchy
of Botany. There also is a number for Natural Science (220.85) as a
topic under the Bible. A church library would certainly want such a
book near similar Bible subjects, such as Children of the Bible.

Check the library's cataloging guidelines for exceptions, such
as how to handle individual biography or fiction. Libraries often
use 920 for collective biography and B for individual biography.
Guidelines help you to be consistent.

Aids to classification. Some of the new books now coming out
have Library of Congress cataloging information printed on the back
of the title page. This is called Cataloging-in-Publication. It
provides the Library of Congress classification number and the Dewey

classification number, as well as subject headings. Juanita Carpenter calls this "one of the fine helps for church librarians." She adds, "You may have wondered why the Dewey number is often broken up by little diagonal marks that resemble an apostrophe. This mark is called a 'prime mark'....It is placed in the number to show librarians where they may properly segment it if they are using an abridged Dewey classification....Cut the classification number at one of the prime marks. Be sure to check your shelf list to see where you have classified like books in your church library and how many digits you previously used."[3]

Another useful aid is the American Book Publishing Record (New York, R.R. Bowker Co., monthly), available in most public libraries. This lists Dewey numbers and subject headings assigned by the Library of Congress. Each month it lists new books that have been published, and it is cumulated annually. The main part is arranged by Dewey number and there are author and title indexes in the back of each issue.

The public-library card catalog is another aid. If the public library has the book, professional classifiers would have assigned a subject number. Check this in your Dewey before you use it, to make sure that it places the book on the shelf where you want it in your subject scheme.

If you really get stuck with a classification problem, call a conference. Talk it over with other church librarians, or the librarian of your public library. You are sure to come up with a suitable number.

With experience comes confidence - so just get in there and do it. You always can readjust and change early decisions if later experiences tell you to. In the meantime, the books can be located on the shelf, you have a record, and the books can be used. Get started and learn as you go.

Forming the Call Number

Within a subject number, there is apt to be more than one book. An author symbol is added after the classification number to give each book an alphabetical sequence on the shelf, within the subject number. The classification number and the author symbol - together - are the book's call number. This call number should be different and distinctive for each book - unless it is an added copy.

The call number locates a specific book in the library, just as a street address locates a specific house in a town. There are no two houses with the exact same street and number. Likewise, there should be no two books in the library with the exact same call number (except the added copies). Duplicate copies or different volumes of the same title are like apartments within an apartment house. Each has the same call number (street address), but each also has a unique accession number, copy number or volume number (apartment number).

Alphabetical symbol. The author symbol is usually the first three letters of the author's last name. Write these letters in pencil under the classification number on the work card. Example: "Jon" for "Jones."

Check the shelf list to make sure the call number thus formed has not been used before. Since the shelf list is arranged by call number, just as the books are arranged on the shelf, you can tell at a glance if the call number is already in use. If it is, erase the author symbol you wrote on the work card and change it just enough to make the call number unique. For example: "Joe" or "Jos" for "Jones." Some libraries use the first letter of the title after the author symbol to vary a call number. Example: "JonT" for a book, _Teaching_ by Jones.

If your library collection is rather large and you have many books within one subject number, you might consider using the Cutter tables for assigning author symbols. These tables arrange numbers after the first letter of the author's last name to keep most English-language names in alphabetical sequence. Public libraries quite often use the Cutter numbers for author symbols. These tables can be purchased through the library-supply catalogs.

Symbols for biography. The author symbol for a biography of an individual is an exception to the general rule for author symbols. Use the first three letters of the subject - the person about whom the biography is written. Example: "B " for a biography of Albert Schweitzer.
                                         Sch

If you have more than one biography of the same person, add the first letter of the author's last name after the chosen symbol.
Example: "B   " "B   "
          SchA (by Anderson),   SchH (by Hagedorn).

Shelf-list marker. Write the call number on a temporary marker and place it in the shelf-list file until the shelf-list card is typed. When the permanent shelf-list card is filed, remove the temporary marker. We find that it helps to add the accession number to the temporary marker to identify the book should the temporary marker not be removed for some reason.

Write the call number in the book itself. Turn to the back of the title page. (Location varies with libraries. Some prefer to use the page facing the back of the title page, or the title page itself.) Write the call number in pencil, about one inch down from the top and one inch away from the inside binding.

Designating Added Entries

How many ways would you like to be able to find the book in your card catalog? Author? Title? Subject? Other?

The main entry card will be filed in the catalog by its top line - usually the author. If you want a card in the file under title, sub-title, joint author, translator, editor, compiler, illustrator, series, etc., list these on the work card so the typist will know to make them.

Title and sub-title. The title has already been written on the work card, below the main-entry top line. So, to indicate on the work card that a title card needs to be typed, merely write a lower-case "t" on the lower half of the work card. If a sub-title card is to be made, write a lower case "t" and follow it with the part of the title that is to be picked up as the added entry. Example: "t: Hymn of healing."

Joint authors, etc. Write these out on the bottom half of the work card, just as they will appear on the added entry card - last name first. Follow the name with a comma and an abbreviated title. Example: "Doulos, Bill Lane, jt. auth."

Subjects. Write the topics for subject cards on the work card - all in capital letters (this helps to remind the typist that they are to be typed that way). Example: "FAMILY LIFE." The selection of subject headings should be done thoughtfully with the users of the catalog in mind.

Selecting Subject Headings

How you choose subject headings is important in making the catalog a useful tool. Each individual book can be shelved in only one place. However, it can be located in many places in the catalog. First, write on the work card the subject that describes the book's primary classification. This part is the easiest. In many cases, that is the only subject card you will wish to make. Example: JESUS CHRIST - CHILDHOOD.

Other subject cards will identify and make accessible additional subject information in the book. Example: PARENT AND CHILD; FAMILY RECREATION. They also can present a subject in an alternative way to increase the chances that it will be located by a reader in his search through the catalog. Example: FAMILY LIFE - FICTION; SCHOOL STORIES.

Authority file. Keep a record of the subject headings you use in the catalog. This reference file is called an authority file. It helps you to be consistent, to use the same word or words for a subject. Example: SENIOR CITIZENS instead of OLD AGE.

Another way of keeping track of subject headings used is to place a pencil check before the subject heading in a printed list, such as Sears List of Subject Headings (Bronx, NY, H. W. Wilson Co., 1977) or Dorothy Kersten's Subject Headings for Church or Synagogue Libraries (Bryn Mawr, PA, Church and Synagogue Library Association, 1977). Collect available subject lists to help you in developing a list of your own.

104

Cross references. Directional cards are helpful in the card catalog (and in the authority file). They are called cross reference cards. A "see" reference refers you from nothing to something - from a place where there are no subject cards to a place where there are. Example: PARTIES see AMUSEMENTS.

A "see also" reference refers you from something to something more - from a place where there are subject cards to another where related material is listed. Example: APOSTLES see also names of individual apostles, i.e. MATTHEW, SAINT.

Not long ago, an adult student asked if our library had a copy of the Torah. A quick check of the catalog found no listing. Yet, I remembered that the local Hebrew Congregation had presented to us a two-volume Old Testament with both English and Hebrew texts. Most certainly that would include the Torah. We looked up the definition of the word in the World Book Encyclopedia under Judaism, and found that Torah was the Hebrew word for the Pentateuch, the first five books of the Old Testament. We found it, quite naturally, with the Bibles, and quietly added another cross-reference card to the catalog.

Familiar usage topics. Subject headings are designed to bring people and books together. It is frustrating to search for a specific or new subject and not find it. Existing subject-heading lists often fall short of the need for current, relevant and familiar subject terms. Most libraries find they still need to change headings to keep pace with the timely needs of users. The following are examples of some of the subject headings "created" by the University of Pittsburgh catalogers:

Hypnotism in athletics

Inner city

Natural childbirth

Negro social workers

Police corruption

Sex discrimination

Soul music

The following are some of the cross references added by the University
of the Pacific:

Body language see Nonverbal communication

Chicanos see Mexican-Americans

Ethnic groups see Minorities

Life styles, alternative see Collective settlements

Dorothy Kanwischer says: "It behooves catalogers to scrap a tunnel vi-
sion and barnacle-encrusted approach to subject headings and plunge into
the right-now world of communes, streakers, and political shenanigans."[4]
Yet we must never throw out the baby with the bath water. Keep that
which is good in the old established subject-heading lists and add that
which is good in the new. Be guided by what Mrs. X and Mr. Y will be
searching for. Try to provide access to it.

All this may make classifying sound difficult. It really is not. In
the majority of cases, the books have a way of falling quite naturally
into a subject niche. Practice and experience help you find that niche.

Over the years I learned quite a lot about cataloging church library
books that I did not learn in library school or from work in other libraries. I learned that classification is a matter of judgment about

where books are located and which numbers should be simplified or extended. For example, in our church library we subdivided MISSIONS (266) by country rather than denomination. We were more interested in the fact that the book covered missions in India than whether missions were Presbyterian, Baptist, or a combination of denominations. We refuse to call them mistakes, however, as long as the books can be located on a shelf and are identified by subject in the card catalog.

Analytics. The added entry that identifies something on specific pages of a book is called an analytic. It might be a play, a short story, a prayer or poem in a collection. It might be a subject - perhaps a simple, concise summary on a topic of interest that would be lost if not indexed separately.

The entry for an analytic might be an author or a title, or a combination of author and title (or title first followed by author) or a subject term - followed by the inclusive pages from the book.

When you examine a book for subject content, be on the lookout for parts that would be of specific interest, such as a chapter on Zen Buddhism, a ceremony for the installation of officers, or instructions on how to make a creche.

Juanita Carpenter says: "The use of analytic cards in your card catalog will make for a handy source of ready reference information and will result in a more complete use of your library resources." She says, "A short account on a topic is often more desirable for a church school teacher or student than an entire book on the subject.... For example, you may have noticed an excellent description of Solomon's temple in a Bible history, or you found the 'Pillars of Islam,' the duties underlying Muslim worship, in a book on world religions. The sort of subject analytics you make will depend on the type of request you get in your church library."[5]

Keeping a perspective. Remember the unique reading needs, habits and abilities of your user community. Use words they will understand. If necessary, lead them to the subject terms you have used by means of directional cards. Example: GENERATION GAP see FAMILY LIFE. Or, include a definition of what the subject covers at the beginning of those subject cards in the catalog. Example:

ETERNITY

    used for books on the philosophical
    concept of eternity. Books dealing
    with the character and form of a
    future life are entered under
    FUTURE LIFE.

Keep in mind that the simplest of directions are the easiest to follow. More than likely your congregation will use the library neither for highly technical nor advanced scholarly research, so make it easy for them to use. Add the detail that will help readers find material, but just enough for that average reader who is searching the catalog alone. Remember the words - clear and simple. (See illustration, following page.)

Prepare catalog cards with neatness and accuracy.

Preparing the Catalog Cards

Once I was told that the important thing about keeping accounts was to have a neat and well-written ledger. You could say the same about a card catalog. The care you take in preparing the catalog cards indicates to the user the care you took in cataloging the books. Uniformity in the cards not only makes the catalog look better, it generates trust and confidence.

Card set. A set of catalog cards includes an author card (to be filed by the author), a title card (to be filed by title) and subject cards (one or more, to be filed by subject). Others may be added. The author card is the master card from which all the other cards are copied. Together, the cards form a set.

Sample Card Set

j394.2   Irion, Ruth Hershey.
  Iri   The Christmas cookie tree. Westminster,
           c1976.

Author card

accession
Number

t.
CHRISTMAS STORIES

Tracing

          The Christmas cookie tree
j394.2   Irion, Ruth Hershey.
  Iri   The Christmas cookie tree. Westminster,
           c1976.

Title card

          CHRISTMAS STORIES
j394.2   Irion, Ruth Hershey.
  Iri   The Christmas cookie tree. Westminster,
           c1976.

Subject card

Tracing. The author card ties the set together. On it are listed all the other cards in the set. This is called the tracing. It is useful when you need to pull the cards to make a correction or to withdraw the book from the collection - you can get them all. The tracing tells you how many cards to look for and just where in the catalog they are filed.

List the tracing on the back of the author card (or the front, if preferred, below the cataloging entry). A lower-case "t" is enough to indicate that a title card is to be made, since the title itself already appears on the card. Subject headings are listed the way they will be typed, in all capital letters. Example:

t.   (for title)

MEDITATIONS   (for subject)

Spacing and punctuation. Standard catalog cards are 3" x 5" in size, with a hole punched at center bottom through which a rod is inserted to hold the cards in the catalog drawer. Uniform spacing on the cards makes them easier for the user to scan. It also produces a neat and organized-looking catalog.

The author entry begins two lines down from the top of the card. This allows space for an added entry to be typed at the top of duplicated cards.

The call number begins two lines down from the top also, and one space from the left edge. The author symbol goes below the class number.

Last Name initial enough

Indentions are the number of typewriter spaces from the left edge
for the main-entry information. Although practice varies from library
to library, a common measure is as follows:

First indention   9 typewriter spaces

Second indention   11 typewriter spaces

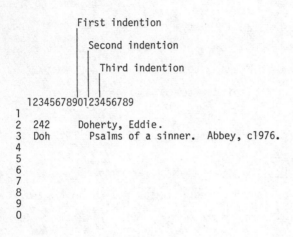

Indentions.

First indention

Second indention

Third indention

```
1234567890123456789
1
2   242     Doherty, Eddie.
3   Doh         Psalms of a sinner.  Abbey, c1976.
4
5
6
7
8
9
0
```

Main-entry card. The author's name begins at the first indention.
Type the author's last name first, followed by a comma and his given
names (or initials). Titles such as "Doctor" or "Professor" are omit-

ted. If the author's name (or other main entry) is so long that it
runs over to the next line, begin the next line at the second indention.
End with a period.

When a title is used as a main entry because the book has no author,
editor, compiler or corporate author, the title begins in the author
position - at the first indention. Capitalize only the first word and
proper names. End with a period. All other lines that follow the title will begin at the second indention. Example:

```
783       At worship; a hymnal for young
Atw           churchmen.  Harper, c1951.
```

The title generally begins on the line below the author (or main
entry), at the second indention. All other lines that follow will begin at the first indention. Example:

```
B         Goudge, Elizabeth.
Gou           The joy of the snow.  Coward McCann,
              c1974.
```

If the sub-title is lengthy, copy just the essential information in the
order in which it appears on the title page. Although not required,
dots may be used to indicate the omissions. Example:

```
220.5     Bible.
Jam           The Holy Bible, containing the Old
              and New Testaments....King James ver-
              sion.  Am. Bible Soc., n.d.
```

Add joint authors, translator, etc., and edition (if other than
the first) directly after the title (or sub-title). Then add the imprint - publisher and date. End with a period. Two lines below this
information, at the second indention, indicate the number of volumes

if more than one.

Two lines below the above, type the notes. Begin at the second indention and continue at the first indention. The individual notes follow each other and each begins at the second indention.

Examples of Main Entries

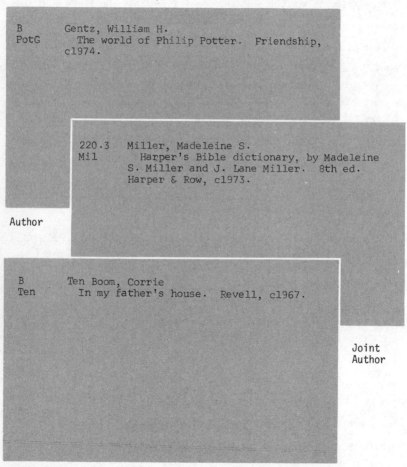

```
B        Gentz, William H.
PotG       The world of Philip Potter.  Friendship,
         c1974.
```

```
220.3    Miller, Madeleine S.
Mil        Harper's Bible dictionary, by Madeleine
         S. Miller and J. Lane Miller.  8th ed.
         Harper & Row, c1973.
```

Author

```
B        Ten Boom, Corrie
Ten        In my father's house.  Revell, c1967.
```

Joint
Author

Compound surname

```
248      Francis de Sales, Saint
Fra          Introduction to the devout life.  Rev.
         ed.  Doubleday, c1972.
```

Forename entries

```
301.4    Evans, Colleen Townsend.
Eva          A new joy.  Guideposts, c1973.

             Bound with: The Christian family, by
         Larry Christenson.  Guideposts, c1970.
```

```
301.4    Christenson, Larry.
Eva          The Christian family.  Guideposts, c1970.

             Bound with:  Evans, C. T.  A new joy.
```

Bound with

```
220.92   Sims, Albert E.      ed.
Sim         Who's who in the Bible.  Ed. by the Rev.
         Albert E. Sims and the Rev. George Dent.
         Philosophical Library, c1960.
```

Editor
as author

```
242      Trueblood, Elton.
Tru         The meditations of Elton Trueblood.
         Ed. by Stephen R. Sebert and W. Gordon
         Ross.  Harper & Row, c1975.
```

Editor NOT as author

```
j200     Life (Periodical)
 Lif        The world's great religions.  Young
         reader's ed.  Golden Press, c1967.
```

Periodical as author

```
225.5   Bible.  New Testament.
Bar         The New Testament; a new translation by
        William Barclay.  Collins, c1969.

            2v.

            Contents:  v.1, The Gospels and the Acts
        of the Apostles; v.2, the Letters and the
        Revelation.
```

Sacred book

```
220.9   National Geographic Society.
Nat         Everyday life in Bible times.  National
        Geographic, c1967.
```

```
641     U. S. Department of Agriculture.  Human
Uni         Nutrition Research Branch.
                Recipes for quantity service.  GPO,
            1954.
```

Corporate
author

Government agency

```
262      Detroit Ordination Conference, Detroit,
Det          MI, 1975.
                Women and Catholic priesthood; an ex-
             panded version.  Ed. by Anne Marie Gar-
             diner.  Paulist Press, c1976.
```

Conference

```
423      Webster's collegiate dictionary.   5th ed.
Web          Merriam, c1941.
```

Title as main entry (no author)

```
296     The Hanukkah anthology.  Comp. by Philip
Han        Goodman.  1st ed.  Jewish Publication
           Society of America., c1976.
```

Compilation

```
283     Episcopal Church Annual.
Epi        Morehouse-Barlow.

           Annual
           Library has

        1975
        1976
        1977
```

Open entry

```
R
016      Audio-visual resources guide.
Aud          Friendship.

             Irregular
             Library has

         9th ed. 1972
```

Frequency and holdings

```
J        Gurley, Jayne.
Gur          The birthday wish.  Illus. by Tom Mas-
             terson.  Revell, c1975.

             Butterfly books (series).
             Grades 1-5.
```

Series and age group

```
025      Media; library services journal (Periodical)
Med         Sunday School Board, Southern Baptist
            Convention.

            Quarterly.

            Preceded by Church library magazine.
```

Title change

```
225      Bible.  N.T.
Dar         The New Testament of our Lord and Savior
         Jesus Christ.  Ed. by Gilbert Darlington.
         Am. Bible Soc., 1955.

            Cover title:  Good news.
```

```
649      Sloane, Valerie.
Slo         Creative family activities.  Abingdon,
         c1976.

            Jacket sub-title:  Living, loving and
         learning together.
```

Cover
title

Jacket sub-title

```
B        Hindman, Jane F.
Neu        An ordinary saint; the life of John
         Neumann.  Arena Lettres, c1977.

           Summary:  A biography of the Bishop
         renowned for his good deeds who was
         proclaimed a saint in 1977.
```

Summary

```
920      Eisenhower, Julie Nixon.
Eis        Special people.  Simon & Schuster, c1977.

           Contents:  Golda Meir.-Ruth Bell Braham.-
         Charles, Prince of Wales.-Anne Morrow Lind-
         berg.-Mao Tse-tung.-Mamie Doud Eisenhower.
```

Contents

Added entries. All added cards are exact duplicates of the main one (author card) except that each has a line added to the top to show where in the catalog it will file.

An added entry begins one line down from the top at the second indention. If it is too long for one line, continue on the next line at the third indention and begin the main entry on the third line instead of the second.

A title card repeats the title on the top line, just as it appears below the author's name. Do not include the sub-title. Capitalize the first word and proper names only. End with a period. A long title can be shortened by inserting dots to show that some of the title has been omitted. In some cases a title card will not be needed at all. For example, a biography or other book with the same title and subject:

John Wesley (title)	Religious education (title)
WESLEY, JOHN (subject)	RELIGIOUS EDUCATION (subject)

When this is the case, most libraries would use only the subject card.

A subject card is a copy of the author card with the subject typed on the top line. Type the subject in all capital letters.

Type an added entry card for each item listed in the tracing. Abbreviate descriptive phrases such as editor, compiler, translator, etc. Example: "Birnbaum, Philip, ed."

Analytic cards. The dictionary says that analytic means "relating to analysis, especially separating something into component parts." Important chapters or parts of a book can be identified by analytic

added entries. The information added to the top of the card might be
one line (an author, a title or a subject) or it may be two lines (an
author and title, or a title and author). Spacing is the same as for
the other added entries -- begin at the second indention and continue
at the third. Analytics are different from other added entries in
that you always show inclusive pages at the end of the entry. Example:
"NOAH'S ARK pp. 95-112."

Examples of Added Entries

```
        The pilgrim's progress from this world
           to that which is to come.
F       Bunyan, John.
Bun       The pilgrim's progress from this world
        to that which is to come; with an intro-
        duction by Samuel McChord Crothers.  Scrib-
        ner's, c1918.
```

Long
  title

```
           Christ's resurrection and Christian
              vocation.
232.9   Minear, Paul S.
Min        To die and to live; Christ's resurrec-
        tion and Christian vocation.  Seabury,
        c1977.
```

Sub-title

124

```
           Richards, Lawrence O.      jt. auth.
268    McDaniel, Elsiebeth.
McD        You and preschoolers, by Elsiebeth
       McDaniel and Lawrence O. Richards.
       Moody, c1976.
```

Joint author

```
           Birnbaum, Philip       ed.
221.5  Bible. O.T.
Bir        The concise Jewish Bible.  Ed. & trans.
       by Philip Birnbaum.  Sanhedrin, c1976.
```

```
           Barclay, William       trans.
226.6  Bible. N.T. Acts.
Bar        The Acts of the Apostles.  Trans. with
       an introduction and interpretation by
       William Barclay.  Rev. ed.  Westminster,
       c1976.
```

Editor

Translator

```
          Zulke, Frank       comp.
300    Through the eyes of social science.  Comp.
Thr       by Frank Zulke.  Kendall Hunt, c1976.
```

Compiler

```
          Karch, Paul        illus.
J      Moore, W. Mark.
Moo       Together with daddy.  Illus. by Paul
       Karch.  Broadman, c1976.

          Summary:  A youngster explains why
       she thanks God for her father.
```

Illustrator

```
          An exploration book.
261    Fahey, Sheila Macmanus.
Fah       Charismatic social action; reflection/
       resource manual.  Paulist, c1977.

          Series:  An exploration book.
```

Series

```
        Rock of ages p.259:
783     Reynolds, William Jensen.
Rey        A survey of Christian hymnody.  Holt,
        Rinehart & Winston, c1963.

           Contains illustrative hymns with music:
        Amazing grace.-Lead kindly light.-Rock of
        ages.-etc.
```

Analytic: Title

```
        LAKE OF GALILEE p.110:
915.6   Hollis, Christopher.
Hol        Holy places; Jewish, Christian and
        Muslim monuments in the Holy Land.  Praeger,
        c1969.

           Contains maps and plans: Jewish holy
        places.-Christian holy places.-Constantinian
        and present day churches of the Nativity,
        Bethlehem.-Church of the Annunciation,
        Nazareth.-The Lake of Galilee.-and others.
```

Analytic: Subject

Examples of Cross References

CHILD PSYCHOLOGY

see

CHILD STUDY

See (from nothing to something)

APOSTLES

see also

names of individual apostles, i.e.
MATTHEW, SAINT.

See also (from something to something more)

<u>Cards, pockets and labels</u>. Include book cards, pockets and labels
as part of the typing process. All the information is at hand and fresh
in mind. The book cards and pockets are spaced identically for easy
matching when the book card is replaced in the pocket. Allow each bit
of information to stand out. Type the call number upper left and the
accession number (or copy number) upper right. Skip a line and type
the author's last name followed on the next line by the title. Example:

```
223                              237
Ter

Terrien
The Psalms and their meaning
   for today
```

For children's books, you might wish to add an age group, below the accession number or below the title. Example:

```
j232              913    j232                        913
  Our                      Our
                  6-9
Oursler                   Oursler
Life of Jesus             Life of Jesus
                          6-9
```

Examples of labels are as follows:

```
                                        R
225      278      262      j232      220       B
Gam      Bar      Edi       Jon      Int       SchW
         v.1      1973                Suppl.
```

Check all typing for accuracy after it is completed.

Shelf-List Record

"I am a great believer in a shelf-list file," writes Rachel Kohl, Chairman of the Library Services Committee of the Church and Synagogue Library Association, "not only as a means of determining where the collection needs building, but for inventory and insurance purposes." She also reports that "one librarian to whom I recommended such a file was able to interest her husband in helping her and they found it guided them in pulling together like material that had been classified in two or more places."[6]

Examples of Shelf-List Cards

```
j394.2    Irion, Ruth Hershey.
  Iri         The Christmas cookie tree.  Westminster,
          c1976.

1395  March 25, 1977
```

```
R
220.3    Interpreter's dictionary of the Bible.
Int          Ed. by George Arthur Buttrick and others.
             Abingdon, c1962.

             4v.

325   v.1  July 31, 1969
326   v.2  July 31, 1969
327   v.3  July 31, 1969
328   v.4  July 31, 1969
762   Suppl.  December 12, 1970
```

The shelf list is just what it says - a list of books as they appear on the shelf. Cards in the shelf list are filed by call number. The shelf-list card is a duplicate of the author card, but it tells how many copies you have, when they were added and - in some cases - where you got them.

Type the accession number two lines down from the body of the card and one space from the left. Some libraries add date received, source and cost. Others merely add the date the book was cataloged. When another copy of the book is received, type the same information for the added copy on the line below the previous accession number.

Adding the score. Keep track of what you have done. Count the number of books you have cataloged. Keep a cataloging record that tells how many books were added during the year and how many are in the total collection. Statistics such as these can be a real asset. They help support future budget requests.

This also is a good time to make a list of the new additions to post in the library, announce in the home newsletter or circulate to the membership as an insert in the worship bulletin. This promotes use of the books.

Filing

"A card misfiled represents an item which is lost to the user of the card catalog," says Marilyn Hager.[7] As in the parable of the lost coin, one can search through the house to find it. Therefore, in order to minimize lost cards, file in a two-step process. One person files the cards, but leaves them above the rods so that they stand a quarter-inch above the other cards. Another person, preferably the cataloger, double-checks the accuracy of the filing, pulls out the rod, and drops the cards into place.

File cards in the catalog in alphabetical order according to what appears on the top line. One integrated alphabetical file is recommended. It saves filing time, typing time (because a title card is not needed if it is the same as the subject card), drawer space, and the time of the user (because he consults one file instead of three).

File cards in the shelf-list file by call number - numerically and then alphabetically. The arrangement of the shelf list is the same as the arrangement of books on the shelf.

Label the drawers so users - library helpers as well as patrons - will know at a glance what each drawer contains.

Filing rules. Consistency in filing is important. Start with a basic set of rules for all to follow. Example:

a. File all cards in one alphabetical arrangement. Example:

Letters   (title)
LOVE   (subject)
Lovejoy   (author)

b. File word by word (nothing comes before something). Example:

Let go and let God

Let God help you

Letter of Paul to the Galatians

Lettering: a guide for teachers

Letters to young churches

c. Ignore "a," "an" or "the" at the beginning of a line (but include it when it appears in the middle of a line). Ignore all punctuation. Example:

CHILD STUDY

The child under six

CHILDREN

Children around the world

CHILDREN - RELIGIOUS LIFE

Children: the challenge

CHILDREN'S SONGS

A child's grace

d. File abbreviations and numbers as though spelled out. Example:

Dr.	doctor	5	five
Mr.	mister	17	seventeen
Mrs.	mistress	100	one hundred
Ms.	mistress	1001	one thousand and one
St.	saint		
U.S.	United States		

e. If several cards have the same author, arrange alphabetically according to the next line (the title). Example:

Tabor, Gladys.
  Country chronicle.

Tabor, Gladys.
  Harvest of yesterdays.

f. If several cards have the same subject, arrange alphabetically according to the next line (the main entry). Example:

    PRAYERS
      Barclay, William.

    PRAYERS
      Boyd, Malcolm.

    PRAYERS
      Harkness, Georgia.

    PRAYERS
      Holmes, Marjorie.

g. If the author and the subject are the same (books by and about the same person), file the author cards before the subject cards. Example:

    Jones, E. Stanley   author

    JONES, E. STANLEY   subject

h. If subject and title cards are the same, file the subject cards before the title cards. (Some libraries like to interfile these alphabetically according to the next line.) Example:

    Religious education   title
      Fox...

    RELIGIOUS EDUCATION   subject
      Trevethan...

<u>Guide cards.</u> Like the thumb tabs on a dictionary, guide cards in the catalog help the user (and the filer) go directly to the section of interest. Insert a guide card for each letter of the alphabet. As the catalog grows, add guide cards for major subject headings as well. File cards in back of the guide cards.

<u>Aids.</u> For additional help in filing, consult references such as

the following at the public library: <u>Akers Simple Library Cataloging</u>
(completely revised and rewritten by Arthur Curley and Jana Varlejs,
6th ed., Metuchen, NJ, Scarecrow Press, 1977), and Esther J. Piercy,
<u>Commonsense Cataloging</u> (Bronx, NY, H. W. Wilson Co., 1965).

Preparing Books for the Shelves

A teacher of mine once referred to this process of preparing materials for use as "marking and parking." Each book is assigned a parking sticker (label) which gives it a place on the shelf. The processing of each book requires stamping, pasting and labeling.

<u>Stamp</u> the name of your library on the title page and some other
page in the book. This other page is the library's secret page and,
usually, is an odd number page. It is the same in each book. Also,
stamp the library name on the book pocket. Some libraries like to
stamp the edges of the pages as well.

<u>Paste</u> the book pocket and due slip in the back of the book. If
the pockets are pasted on the page facing the inside of the back cover,
they do not interfere with the plastic jacket cover. This also relieves
the cover of that added weight and prolongs the life of the binding
hinge. Place the pocket near the bottom of the page and the date slip
near the top. In small books, the bottom of the date slip can be tucked
inside the pocket. Place the book card in the pocket.

<u>Label</u> the book by lettering the call number directly on the spine
of the book or by affixing a label on which the call number has been
lettered. (See Chapter 4.)

261   Christian Church

Book labels form a neat, straight eye-line on the shelf.

The label should always be placed the same distance from the bottom of the book, such as 1" or 1½" up. The book labels will form a
neat, straight line when the books are on the shelf - not a jagged,
up-and-down hop-skip-jump. This makes it easier for the searcher to
read across, and keeps the shelves looking neat and cared for.

Make a measuring gauge. Cut a piece of cardboard like a small
frame that measures 1" (or whatever distance you decide) on all sides,
or use a 1" strip. Stand the book upright and place the cardboard
against the spine. Draw a light pencil mark on the spine to indicate
the location of the bottom of the label.

Numbers and letters should be large and legible, so that they
can be seen when the book is on the shelf. Type the labels or use a
permanent black ink (or use a stylus and transfer paper directly on

the spine). One library I know places a piece of permanent mending tape across the ink label (after the ink is dry) to hold it more firmly in place and protect the lettering.

Very thin books and pamphlets have little if any space on the spine for a label. Place the label on the front cover, 1" down and in from the top left corner. Since most people begin to remove a book by placing a finger at the top of the spine and tipping it forward, the label is quickly visible. However, some libraries prefer to place all labels the same distance from the bottom of the book - even those on the front cover.

Oversize books usually are filed on a separate shelf, away from their normal numerical location, to make the best use of overall space. Label "dummy" markers to file in their place on the regular shelf. A good dummy marker can be made from ½" plywood, cut to standard book size and varnished. Place a strip of Mystic tape along one long edge to serve as a spine, if desired. Label the dummy with the call number of the book and add a note to "see oversize shelf." This helps people to help themselves.

Cover jacket. "Transparent vinyl, acetate, or mylar covers may be put on over the jackets of books...," affirms Mildred L. Nickel. "These keep the materials clean, protect them from wear, and invite use."[8] These covers extend the shelf life of a book and often eliminate the need for rebinding. Further, they do not become brittle and can be wiped clean when soiled.

Measure the height of the book in inches. Select a plastic cover that will fit. When in doubt, choose a larger cover, as a crowded fit will wrinkle the paper jacket. Fit the plastic cover over the book's paper cover and replace it on the book. Some covers come equipped with self-adhesive strips that fasten it to the book. Otherwise, fasten the jacket cover to the book with permanent mending tape. Avoid using cellophane tape, as it will yellow, crack and peel off in time, leaving an unsightly mark in its place. Permanent mending tape will not do this. It will remain like new throughout the life of the jacket.

Shelve the books as a final step. Arrange them numerically according to classification number, beginning with 000, reading left to right and top to bottom within each section of shelving. Try not to fill each shelf full, but leave "working space" for books to be added. This saves having to shift the books often. Shelve children's books apart from the adult books. Place fiction either at the beginning or the end of the classified numbers. Individual biography classed "B" usually comes at the end. Reference books and oversize books (so marked on the label) are placed on a shelf of their own.

Shortcuts in Cataloging

Help for cataloging specific books is available, if you know where to find it. Printed catalog cards, commercial processing services and other aids provide shortcuts in cataloging.

Cataloging-in-publication. Look on the back of the title page of the book. More and more publishers are including information supplied by the Library of Congress. This is in the form of a preliminary main-entry card, with suggested LC number, Dewey number and subject headings.

LC cards. Sets of catalog cards are available for purchase from the Library of Congress. These printed cards have more information than the average church or synagogue library needs, but they have a standard printed format and are authoritative. The receiving library must type in the call number and all added entries. However, both LC and Dewey numbers are suggested, along with subject headings and other added entries. An order for cards is processed more quickly if you supply the order number for the card set. This usually is printed on the back of the title page as follows: "Library of Congress Catalog Card No. 65-24135."

Examples of LC Printed Cards

U. S. *Dept. of State.*
 The U. S. Department of State fact book of the countries of the world. Introd. by Gene Gurney. New York, Crown ₁1970₁

 702 p. illus., maps., ports. 28 cm. 5.95
 Includes bibliographies.

 1. World politics—1965– 2. Almanacs, American. ɪ. Title.
ɪɪ. Title: Fact book of the countries of the world.

D849.U55 1970   910   70–113400
                    MARC

Library of Congress   70 ₁4₁

Meyer, Roger E
 Guide to drug rehabilitation; a public health approach, by Roger E. Meyer. Foreword by Jerome H. Jaffe. Boston, Beacon Press ₁1972₁

 xv, 171 p. 21 cm. $5.95
 Title on spine: Guide to drug rehabilitation; a public health response.
 Bibliography: p. ₁155₁–167.

 1. Drug abuse—Treatment. 2. Narcotic addicts—Rehabilitation. ɪ. Title.

HV5801.M47   362.2'93   76–179152
ISBN 0–8070–2772–3   MARC

Library of Congress   72 ₁4₁

<u>Commercial services</u> save cataloging time. While some companies offer printed card sets, others offer complete processing - cards along with labeling, pasting pockets and affixing jacket covers. Quite often these services are tied in with the purchase of books. Many of the companies offering such services deal primarily in books for school libraries and would not be expected to carry many religious titles. However, there are dealers who offer cards with or without purchases and can supply them for most of the general books in print.

In general, commercial processing services provide Dewey and Sears cataloging - the classification numbers from the abridged Dewey and subject headings from the Sears subject heading list. Catalog-card kits include a set of catalog cards (and a shelf-list card), with call number and added entries in place at the top, plus a book card, pocket and label. Complete processing includes the catalog-card kits, plus the label on the book, book pocket pasted in place, and a jacket cover attached. Options are offered by some companies which allow you to take all or only a part of these services and to designate variations in the simplified Dewey call numbers, such as how many letters of the author's last name below the classification number. Some typical services are listed below:

American Econo-clad Services
507 Jackson
Topeka, KA 66612

Card kits or complete processing, with book orders from their catalog. Mostly children's books.

Associated Libraries, Inc.
229 North 63rd Street
Philadelphia, PA 19139

Card kits or complete processing, with book orders from
their catalog. Options available on cards.

The Baker & Taylor Company

Eastern Division
50 Kirby Avenue
Somerville, NJ 08876

Southwest Division
Industrial Park
Clarksville, TX 75426

Southeast Division
Commerce, GA 30529

Western Division
380 Edison Way
Reno, NV 89502

Midwest Division
Gladiola Avenue
Momence, IL 60954

This company is a book-ordering service and does not issue
a catalog of available titles. Card kits or complete processing services are available with orders for most books
in print. Options available. They offer either abridged
Dewey and Sears, unabridged Dewey and LC subject headings,
or LC classification and subject headings.

Follett Library Book Company
4506 Northwest Highway (Route 14 and 31)
Crystal Lake, IL 60014

Card kits or complete processing services, with books ordered
from their catalog. Options available.

Huntting
300 Burnett Road
Chicopee, MA 01020

Card kits or complete processing services available with orders for most books in print. A minimum of 25 books is required.

Josten's
Library Services Division
1301 Cliff Road
Burnsville, MN 55337

Catalog-card kits or complete processing for most books in
print (including paperbacks). The card kits are available
with or without book orders. Options available. (See sample
cards at end of list.)

Metro Litho
900 North Franklin Street
Chicago, IL 60610

Catalog-card kits or complete processing services for publishers and distributors. No custom options. High-quality
printing.

Xerox Bibliographics
LJ Cards Department
2500 Schuster Drive
Cheverly, MD 20781

Catalog-card kits. No book orders. Components not sold
separately. Cards available for most juvenile titles in
print, some young adult and reference books.

Examples of Library-Service Card Kits

```
634      Silverstein, Alvin
Si          Apples: all about them, by Alvin
         Silverstein and Virginia B. Silverstein.
         Illus. by Shirley Chan.  Prentice 1976
          112p  illus  bibl
           634
```

FRUIT

| 634 | Silverstein, Alvin |
| Si | Apples: all about them, by Alvin |

634 Silverstein, Alvin
Si   Apples: all about them, by Alvin
Silverstein and Virginia B. Silverstein.
Illus. by Shirley Chan. Prentice 1976
112p illus bibl

Describes the history of and legends
about the apple, its cultivation, games,

APPLE

634 Silverstein, Alvin
Si   Apples: all about them, by Alvin
Silverstein and Virginia B. Silverstein.
Illus. by Shirley Chan. Prentice 1976
112p illus bibl

Describes the history of and legends

Apples

634 Silverstein, Alvin
Si   Apples: all about them, by Alvin
Silverstein and Virginia B. Silverstein.
Illus. by Shirley Chan. Prentice 1976
112p illus bibl

634 Silverstein, Alvin
Si   Apples: all about them, by Alvin
Silverstein and Virginia B. Silverstein.
Illus. by Shirley Chan. Prentice 1976
112p illus bibl

Describes the history of and legends
about the apple, its cultivation, games,
crafts, and recipes.

1. Apple 2. Fruit I. Title

634
Si

634   Silverstein, Alvin
Si
        Apples

634   Silverstein, Alvin
Si
        Apples

DATE	ISSUED TO

This is a sample of the materials
used in preparing a fully processed book.

*   *   *

Catalog card sets ordered separately or with books
do not include pockets and book cards which may be
ordered from Josten's Library Supplies catalog.

One must be cautious about purchasing cards with pre-selected classifications. What seems like a short cut might not really be one. For example, the classification numbers or the subject headings already chosen and printed on the cards might not be suitable for your collection. Bernard Polishuk confirms this when he says: "At face value, it would certainly seem most economical to purchase catalog cards for all books ordered. However, one problem arises....I often find the tracings on some of the cards so inappropriate, that it is not practical for me to use them in the card catalog...." The card with the unsuitable tracing must be retyped or a line drawn through the added entry which produces a messy card.[9] There are alternative shortcuts.

American Book Publishing Record (New York, R.R. Bowker Co., monthly) lists all the new trade books published in the United States and includes the Dewey numbers and subject headings assigned by the Library of Congress. It does not include government publications or pamphlets under 49 pages, and sometimes overlooks denominational publications because the publishers did not provide information to LC for cataloging. However, it does include the majority of new books on the market.

The main section is arranged by subject, according to Dewey classification. There are alphabetical author and title indexes in the back. Each year the monthly listings are put together in an annual cumulated volume. This makes it faster to search. All you need to know is the year that the book was published. Most public libraries subscribe to this service.

Other aids. Look for book-review sections in denominational or library periodicals, such as Church and Synagogue Libraries (Bryn Mawr, PA, Church and Synagogue Library Association, bimonthly). For older books, similar information is available in references such as the Book Review Digest which usually is in the public library. Remember, too, that the public library has a religion collection. Check their card catalog. Ask the librarian for tips on possible new sources of such information.

Automation. If yours is a particularly progressive public library, chances are they will be connected by computer to a store of bibliographic information, such as the Ohio College Library Center (OCLC) and can obtain cataloging information by communicating with the computer from a keyboard terminal something like a typewriter. Each library pays for its "on-line connect time" but information is transmitted in seconds and is displayed on a television-type screen (cathode ray tube) or may be printed out on an attached printer (like a teletype machine). Networks like this are growing. Someday soon, access will be inexpensive enough that the average church or synagogue library will have a terminal of its own. By typing just the International Standard Book Number (ISBN) which appears on the back of the title page, a distant computer will provide complete cataloging information. If asked, the system will provide a complete set of tailored catalog cards for your use, and these will arrive through the mail. Only the larger libraries are doing these things today, but soon the smaller ones will find it economical enough to join the network.

The library of tomorrow will not have a card catalog at all, but will communicate with its own mini-computer to display on a television screen the catalog-card information, an abstract (summary of contents), or a view of the complete contents of the book page by page.

7/ Cataloging Maps, Pamphlets and Clippings

In planning our new library, we wanted to make the best use of
space. So we purchased a card catalog with a four-drawer legal-size
file unit beneath it - two drawers high and two drawers wide. This
provided a place to file material of temporary value, such as small
pamphlets, clippings and maps. It became the "vertical file" - also
known as an "information file" or "pamphlet file." The name vertical
file stems from the fact that it generally stands upright, like an
office filing cabinet.

Organizing a Vertical File

Since current topics often are discussed in magazines, newspapers
and pamphlets before they appear in books, a vertical file supplements
the book collection. Pamphlets and clippings often add subjects that
otherwise would not be covered. Maps - many of which are large enough
to be posted - extend the atlas collection.

Collect material. Be alert for useful vertical-file material.
Look through those old issues of periodicals. Sort the "junk mail"
that comes in. Get on the mailing list of foundations and other organizations which issue useful free and inexpensive material. Government publications are a good source, too. For example, the Consumer
Information Center (Pueblo, CO 81009) issues a free "Consumer Information Catalog" of selected federal publications of consumer interest.

Among the free titles listed in the Winter 1977-78 issue are "Feeding the Sick Child," "How to Talk to Your Teenager About Drinking and Driving," and "Consumer Guide for Older People."

Separate the materials of lasting value and catalog them along with the books. File the other material in large manila envelopes or folders, by subject. This material in folders need not be accessioned.

Choose subjects based on the current interests of the congregation. Although many of the subject headings will be the same as those used in the card catalog, current topics - too new to have been incorporated in a subject-heading list - will have to be added. For example, we had a folder in the vertical file on DEAD SEA SCROLLS long before the first book was written. Current catch-phrases and the popular names for discussion topics are quite acceptable subject headings in a vertical file.

Label the folders by typing or writing the subject in ink in all capital letters. Locate the label in the same place on each folder - on the pre-cut tab or in the upper right corner. Stick-on labels keep the file looking uniform and neat. File the folders alphabetically by subject.

Preparing the Material

Take time to prepare the material that will go into each folder.

The file must not become a casual dumping ground. The material that goes into it should be screened for usefulness and then properly prepared.

Pamphlets. Stamp the library's name in the pamphlet as if it were a book. Some libraries also stamp the date received, so material that is not used over a period of time can be identified and weeded out. Letter the subject on the pamphlet, such as the upper left corner. Add the type of material after the subject. Example: "MIDDLE EAST - pamphlet." This will identify it as an item from the vertical file and will distinguish it from other items charged out from the same subject folder. No charge card or pocket is necessary. A handwritten charge is prepared at the time the material circulates, since an item from the folder or the entire folder might be taken out at one time.

Clippings. Make sure that clippings are neatly trimmed. On the margin, write in ink the source, date and page(s). Some libraries like to mount clippings on a sheet of paper with just a daub of library paste or permanent mending tape. Others insert them in plastic sheet protectors. The nature of the clipping (from a newspaper or from a glossy magazine) will help you determine if a clipping needs such protection. Stamp the library's name wherever there is room, perhaps on the back. Also letter the subject as above. Example: "MIDDLE EAST - clipping."

150

Look for the title on a map to establish its main entry.

Maps. Fold a large map so the legend is visible. Reinforce fold lines by adding a strip of permanent mending tape or masking tape on the back. Some libraries also place a strip of tape at the bottom and top of the back, to reinforce those that are meant to be posted. Make sure the date of the map is apparent. If necessary, write the date in parentheses after the title. Letter the subject near the legend. If a stick-on label is used, be sure that it does not obscure valuable information. Example: "MIDDLE EAST - map."

Typing Catalog Cards

Although not required, some libraries like to make catalog cards for vertical-file material. Others merely make a list of the subjects and prepare cross-reference cards for the catalog, to lead readers to the folders in the vertical file.

151

<u>Cross references.</u> If there is no other material listed in the catalog under the subject, make a "see" reference (from nothing to something). If there are books listed under the same subject, use a "see also" reference (from something to something more) and file it at the beginning of the subject cards in the catalog.

Sample Cross-Reference Cards

MORMON TABERNACLE
    see
vertical file.

ARTS AND CRAFTS
    see also
    vertical file.

See

See also

Vertical-file catalog cards. Although it is not required, you may decide to catalog individual items in the vertical file. Use "VF" as the call number on the catalog cards (not on the labels). Some libraries use "P" or "Pam." for the pamphlets, "C" or "Clip." for the clippings and "M" or "Map" for the maps. After the title, insert the type of material in parentheses. Add the following note to each card: "Filed in vertical file under [subject]."

Sample Vertical-File Catalog Cards

VF   Ott, Helen Keating.
           Helping children through books; a
        selected booklist for the seventies.
        (Pamphlet) Church and Synagogue Library
        Association, 1974.

           Filed in vertical file under CHILDREN'S
        LITERATURE.

Pamphlet -
author main
entry

VF   Our thanks to (Joe) Josephine. (Pamphlet)
           Philadelphia-Baltimore Conference, Union
        Wesley A. M. E. Zion Church, Washington,
        D. C., September 10, 1976.

           Includes biographical sketch.
           Filed in vertical file under KYLES,
        DR. JOSEPHINE H.

Pamphlet - title main entry

```
VF          Volunteers.  (Newspaper clipping)  The
            Washington Star, December 7, 1977.

            Lists opportunities for volunteer service.
            Filed in vertical file under VOLUNTEER
            SERVICE.
```

```
VF          Valente, Judith.
              Hanukah; young celebrate ancient rite.
            (Newspaper clipping)  The Washington Post,
            December 5, 1977.

              With picture.
              Filed in vertical file under HANUKAH.
```

Clipping -
title main
entry

Clipping - author main entry

```
VF          Land of the Bible today.  (Map)  National
            Geographic Society, 1976.

            1 sheet, color, 41 x 29 in.

            Scale:  1 in. = 45 in.
            Includes notes on Biblical events.
            Filed in vertical file under MIDDLE EAST.
```

Map - title main entry

Collecting Current Archives

The assembling of pamphlets and clippings for the vertical file just naturally led us to collecting current archives. The clippings about the church or the congregation, current pamphlets and leaflets put out by the church, and photographs of major events started out as part of the vertical file. Before long, we realized that this material had more lasting value and should be preserved.

Certain records, such as membership rolls and records of marriages, etc., are kept by the organization's office. Yet, other church history often is lost because it is not recognized as such while it is happening.

Look for material. Be on the lookout for things to save - church newsletters, programs of special events, booklets, leaflets, membership handbooks, worship bulletins, clippings for the scrapbook, pictures, etc. Collect them in one place. Remember that individual groups have records, too - the choir, the women's society, the youth group, etc. Save all the potential history that passes through your hands.

Help to preserve it. Coordinate with the church-history committee. Undoubtedly they have an ongoing program for preserving the archives. Help them to complete the files. Offer to bind the church newsletter and keep it in the library. Let them know of your willingness to keep the scrapbook up to date or to mount photographs in an album with page protectors. Suggest to them that some photographs, especially the early ones, deserve to be mounted or framed. (See Chapter 8.)

155

Keeping Track of Periodicals

Periodicals are not classified unless they are bound into volumes. As bound volumes they are treated as books. Current issues are checked in as they arrive - on a periodical record card kept in the shelf-list file.

Current issues. Some libraries like to keep track of current subscriptions on an accession sheet, even though an accession number is not assigned. This is a handy all-in-one-place record that tells when you placed the subscription and when it will expire. Use one line of the accession record to fill in date placed, title, source, length of subscription, price and date of expiration. Then, prepare a periodical check-in card to record each issue as it is received.

Look on the contents page of the periodical to find the volume and issues number. Write the issues number or make a check in the appropriate box as each issue comes in.

Sample Check-In Cards

Name																								No. Copies				Expires		
	1	2	3	4	5	6	7	8	9	10	11	12	13	14	15	16	17	18	19	20	21	22	23	24	25	26	27	28	29	30	31
jan.																															
Feb.																															
Mar.																															
Apr.																															
May																															
June																															
July																															
Aug.																															
Sept.																															
Oct.																															
Nov.																															
Dec.																															
	1	2	3	4	5	6	7	8	9	10	11	12	13	14	15	16	17	18	19	20	21	22	23	24	25	26	27	28	29	30	31

Daily or weekly

Name										Due			
Year	Vol.	Jan.	Feb.	Mar.	Apr.	May	June	July	Aug.	Sept.	Oct.	Nov.	Dec.	T.P.&I.

No. Copies

Monthly or less frequently

Stamp the library's name on the cover and on the contents page. Although some libraries like to use plastic covers for periodicals (available from library-supply dealers), this is not really needed unless you expect vigorous use of the magazine. No cards or pockets need be prepared. Charge cards are made out when the item circulates.

Arrange the issues alphabetically by title on the shelf. Display them on sloping shelves, store them flat or shelve them upright in pamphlet boxes. Since most current subscriptions have little permanent value, keep them a year or two if you have space. Then screen them for articles that might still be useful in the vertical file before the issues are discarded.

Bound volumes. Some magazines do have more permanent value in the library and need to be kept. Arrange the issues in chronological order. Store them in pamphlet boxes labeled to indicate contents, or tie them up as complete sets with elastic cord.

Have the complete sets bound for greatest permanence. Check to be sure that all issues of the periodical volume are together. Look in the last issue of the year for a title page and an annual index. If no title page has been included, type one: title, volume number and inclusive dates. Place the issues in the exact order in which they are to be bound, with the first number on top. Place the title page at the beginning and the annual index at the end. Tie these together in a binding package. Give the binder complete instructions as to the type of binding, color, lettering, etc. If other volumes have previously been bound, include a pencil tracing of the lettering.

Bound volumes are cataloged much like books. Stamp the library's name on the title page. Assign an accession number - either from the accession record for books or from a separate accession number series for periodicals. If the latter, the numbering series would begin with "Per" for periodical. Example: "Per-1."

Some libraries classify bound volumes of periodicals and shelve them along with the books in the various subject areas. Others file them on the shelf alphabetically by title. I prefer the alphabetical arrangement, which allows them to be shelved near the current issues.

Catalog cards for periodicals. Unbound periodicals seldom are cataloged, but some libraries do add a cross-reference card to the catalog, under title. This lets readers know that the library has a subscription.

158

Sample Periodical Cross-Reference Card

Christian Herald

see

current periodical shelf.

"See" reference

Bound volumes need a complete set of catalog cards. They may
be accessioned like a book or assigned a number from a series that
begins with "Per" or "Periodical." Example: "Per-1," "Per-2," etc.
The main entry, in most cases, is the title. If the title of the
periodical has changed, use the most recent title and explain former
titles in the notes. When the title history is lengthy, you might
need to use a second card.

In order to keep the two cards together in the file, tie them with
sewing thread. Place a pencil along the bottom of the cards just below
the holes. Tie the thread through the holes and around the pencil.
When the pencil is removed, there will be slack enough in the thread to
allow the cards to be used flexibly, even though they are tied together.
Should the cards need to be pulled, the tie makes sure you get them both.
Also, they are less likely to become separated in the files.

Use the note "title varies" as an alternative to listing former
titles.

Sample Periodical Catalog Cards

Per   Media; library services journal (Periodi-
       cal) Sunday School Board, Southern Bap-
       tist Convention.

       Quarterly.
       Former title: Church library magazine.
       Library has

       1976
       1977

Main entry - no classification number

R
050   The messenger...(card 2)
Mes

       Title varies: 1960-1963, Bethesda Metho-
       dist messenger; 1963-1964, News from church
       to home; 1964-1969, Bethesda Methodist mes-
       senger; 1969-1970, Bethesda United Methodist
       messenger; 1970-1971, The Bethesda messen-
       ger: 1971-   The messenger.

       R
       050   The messenger (Periodical) Bethesda United
       Mes   Methodist Church.

              Monthly, except July and August.
              Library has

              1960-1961   1967-1972
              1961-1962   1973-1975
              1962-1963
              1963-1966
              1966-1967

                                (continued on next
                                     card)

Second
card

Main entry - with classification number

160

```
t:   The Bethesda messenger
t:   Bethesda Methodist messenger
t:   Bethesda United Methodist messenger
t:   News from church to home
```

Tracing

```
R          The Bethesda messenger.
050        The messenger (Periodical)  Bethesda Uni-
Mes            ted Methodist Church.

           (See main card for library holdings)
```

Added-entry card

```
R
050        The messenger (Periodical)  Bethesda Uni-
Mes            ted Methodist Church.

1917   1960-1961  May 17, 1961
2156   1961-1962  September 14, 1963
2157   1962-1963  September 14, 1963
2603   1963-1966  December 12, 1966
2910   1966-1967  March 25, 1968
3027   1967-1972  July 31, 1972
3130   1973-1975  October 18, 1975
```

Shelf-list card

8/ Cataloging
Pictures and Art Prints

"I need a picture of a turkey," the young teacher said as she came into the library, "something the children can trace." Fortunately, we had a picture file. In it were all sorts of Thanksgiving pictures, including some line drawings of turkeys which were saved from the top of a calendar.

Pictures come in many sizes and shapes: cardboard cut-outs, clippings from calendars and magazines, greeting cards, teaching picture sets, posters, photographs, etc. Some of them are works of art - original paintings or duplicated copies worthy of careful preservation.

Most denominational publishing houses include picture sets with the curriculum materials. Teachers and other study-group leaders find these visual aids helpful in presenting the lessons. Pictures of better quality, such as works of art and banners, can be used to enhance the worshipful atmosphere in special rooms or hallways. Individual parishioners can borrow them to enjoy at home.

Unframed small pictures are best handled by filing them like the vertical file - by subject. Some libraries actually incorporate these pictures into the vertical file. Others like to keep them as a separate file. Framed works of art and large mounted pictures require separate storage and generally are valuable enough to catalog. The informational picture file is arranged by subject. The art-picture file is arranged by artist.

Store unframed small pictures in a vertical file.

The Informational Picture File

A collection of teaching pictures is a must. Along with those that come in with the curriculum materials, be on the lookout for useful pictures from other sources. Teachers quite often ask for material on the family going to church, the sacraments, and Biblical homes, cutoms, etc. They also ask for pictures of neighborhood helpers (police, mailmen, teachers, etc.), the seasons and holidays.

163

Many such pictures can be found in magazines, calendars, greeting cards, photographs, coloring books and catalogs. Sometimes stores that carry teaching or art supplies have pictures that are suitable for the church library picture file. For pictures of countries in the current mission studies, ask your local travel bureau for posters or travel brochures and look through old issues of the National Geographic magazine picked up at a garage sale, the thrift shop, or a used-book sale.

Mount pictures. Most pictures are best when mounted. Especially if you expect the pictures to be used more than once, mounting reduces wear and tear. Mounted pictures are easier to file and easier to use, too.

There are various weights of paper and cardboard materials that make suitable picture mounts - from lightweight construction paper to heavy cardboard. Pictures of more permanent value should be given more permanent mounting.

Construction or art paper is an easy, lightweight mount. Choose a color that blends with or contrasts attractively with the colors in the picture. Trim the picture, if needed, to make it look neat. Use a daub of library paste behind each corner of the picture, or a small loop of permanent mending tape (sticky side out), to hold it in place.

Cardboard - from shirt cardboard to poster board - provides a sturdier mount. However, regular mounting board, available from most art-supply stores, is the most durable. Some libraries laminate pictures on the mounting boards for further permanence.

Marking. Teaching pictures are most useful filed by subject. Write on each picture the subject heading under which it will be filed. Some libraries write this on the bottom left corner in front if it is not already printed there. Others write it in small, neat letters on the front of the mounting board in the upper right corner as the picture rests in the file. Still others prefer to affix a subject label on the back of the picture, similar to the folders in the vertical file. Smaller pictures with the same subject can be kept in a folder, in which case the folder also is labeled. Be sure to stamp the library's name on the back of the picture, too.

Adequate markings on the pictures in the file help the teachers and leaders find the ones they need. They also help to put pictures back in file when they are returned from circulation.

Catalog cards for the picture file. Although it is not necessary to make catalog cards for the individual pictures in the informational picture file, it is useful to place a card in the catalog for each subject folder. If there is no other material in the catalog under the subject, make a "see" reference. If there is, make a "see also" reference.

The Art-Picture File

"A church should no more think of trying to get along without colored reproductions of great religious pictures that it would deny itself the use of great hymns, anthems, symbols, architecture, or

Sample Picture-File Cross-Reference Cards

CHURCH ATTENDANCE

see

picture file.

BAPTISM

see also

picture file.

"See"
reference

"See also" reference

ceremonies," says Imo Ruyle Foster. "It takes work to build a picture
collection, but every church should put forth the effort to provide
itself with this resource for inspiration, worship and teaching."[1]

Mounting and Framing. Large reproductions should be mounted
and/or framed in an art shop. (Some are available for purchase
already framed.) They should be mounted on strong mounting board
before being framed (to keep them from wrinkling or warping) and art
shops have the necessary equipment to do this.

166

Small prints can be mounted by amateurs with some measure of success. Mounting boards come in several sizes. They, along with the cements and glues, are available at art-supply stores. Place the picture so that the side margins are equal and the bottom margin is slightly wider than the one at the top. After the glue is dry, some libraries protect both the print and the border around the print by spraying the picture with clear plastic. Thus protected, it can be framed without glass, as long as the frame itself is sturdy enough to hold the picture flat and secure. Make sure the color and texture of a frame complement the picture and show it off to best advantage.

Cataloging art pictures. Framed works of art and prints usually are valuable enough to warrant cataloging. Set up a separate accession record and start the number with the letters "PF" for picture file. Example: "PF-1," "PF-2," etc.

The main entry for an original work of art or an exact reproduction is the name of the artist; for study prints or other graphic material, it is the title. Add the word "picture" in parentheses after the title in both cases. Indicate publisher and date. Then, give the number of pictures in the set (if applicable), color and size (in inches), and tell whether it is mounted or framed. Explain in the notes whether it is original art, an art print, photograph, poster, etc., and where it is filed.

Sample Catalog Cards For Pictures

PF Bosch, Hieronymus.
   Adoration of the Magi. (Picture) Arthur
  Rothmann Fine Arts, n.d.

   1 print, color, 22 x 17 in., framed.

   Reproduction.
  Filed in picture file under BOSCH.

Art reproduction

PF Raising of the steeple. (Picture) Edited
   by Stewart H. Webster. Rodney Grantham,
  1968.

   4 photographs, b&w, 8 x 11 in., mounted.

   With typewritten notes.
  Filed in picture file under CHURCH
  HISTORY.

Set of prints

Marking. Since most cataloged pictures will be mounted on heavy cardboard or framed with a cardboard backing, paste a book pocket on the back of each. Type the same information on the card and pocket - accession number, artist and title. Example:

PF-16

Van Gogh
Starry night (Picture)

Be sure to stamp the library's name on the back of the picture as a mark of ownership.

Filing and Storing Pictures

Arrange informational pictures alphabetically by subject in a file cabinet large enough to hold them without folding. Some churches use a large cardboard carton. (Dress it up by covering the outside with construction paper, wallpaper or Contac paper - or simply paint it in a bright color. Paste on a few attractive pictures.) Metal picture cabinets or bins that open from the top generally are available from the denominational supply sources. These allow the pictures to be filed vertically.

Large pictures, posters and framed art usually require separate storage. Hang them on wall hooks in a storage area or place them in a large bin, preferably one with traveling picture rests that help hold them upright in file.

Mount Olivet Lutheran Church Library (Minneapolis, MN) has an outstanding collection of art masterpiece reproductions. These are framed and stored for display in a set of sliding pegboard panels. The pictures circulate to parishioners and their librarian estimates that over half the collection is on loan at all times.[2]

Banners

Banners create a special problem of their own because, generally, they are constructed of cloth. The background fabric, says Rose Mary Ulland, may be "burlap or felt, upholstery or drapery fabric, oil cloth or vinyl, linen or cotton, or any number of fabrics strong enough to support what is to be attached to the surface."[3] Felt, applique, yarns, braids, fringe, buttons, bells, fur, sequins, tapes, pearls, ribbons, feathers, weeds and other objects have been used effectively with banners. The pieces are glued or sewed securely into place.

If banners are folded, the creases are difficult to remove. If they are rolled, the pasted-on figures tend to come off or remain curled when the banner is unrolled. Like framed pictures, they are best stored hanging, on the wall or in a rack of rods.

Most banners are tacked or stapled to the back of a dowel or piece of molding. Woven cord or a leather thong fastens to the end for hanging. Sometimes an upright pole is fastened or clamped to the rod and/or the center of the cord so it can be carried.

Storage. Small banners can be stored like large pictures on

170

flat plywood shelves. Protect them with tissue paper or plastic. Take care that whatever is placed on top will not damage the fabric or the things attached to the banner. It is best to store them on a shelf of their own.

Banners too large to be stored on a shelf should be left hanging, preferably with a covering, like a formal gown on a hanger. If you have a number to store, construct a banner rack. As the collection grows, consider building a mothproof storage closet.

Arrangement. A small collection needs no special arrangement because you can see at a glance what is there. As it grows, you probably will begin to group banners by season of the church year (like clothes in the closet) or to arrange them by general topic, such as BAPTISM. If so, label the banners by subject with a stick-on label in a lower corner on the back.

Cataloging. Cataloging is not required, but it helps program planners to know what is available. At least add a reference card to the card catalog (see sample below). If you decide that full cataloging would be helpful, use the title (caption) as the main entry. If it has no title, make one up and enter it on the catalog card in brackets (or parentheses if your typewriter has no brackets). Follow the title with the word "banner" in parentheses. If known, record who made the banner and when (date). Add size in inches. Record where it is filed in the notes. Example: "Filed in banner file under EASTER." If you keep an accession record, assign a number from the series that begins with "Ban." Example: "Ban-1," "Ban-2," etc.

Sample Catalog Cards for Banners

HOLY SPIRIT
    see

Banner file.

                MUSIC

                    see also

                Banner file.

"See" reference
(if not
cataloged)

            "See also" reference (if not cataloged)

Ban   Joy to the world. (Banner) Designed by
              Judy O'Brien. Made by the Senior High
           class. Bethesda Church, 1976.

              1 banner, color, 36 × 108 in.

              Represents the Christ child in a manger
           setting.
              Filed in banner file under CHRISTMAS.

        Main entry (if cataloged)

9/ Cataloging Film-Type Media

Five minutes before show time. Would enough people come? Had we overlooked something? The feature was <u>The Robe</u>, a full-length Hollywood movie. Although there was no admission charge for viewing it in our church Fellowship Hall, we had hoped to take in enough in voluntary contributions to pay for the rental. Was the gamble worth it - the advance preparation, posted notices on bulletin boards, flyers sent home with the children, letters to other churches in the area, telephone calls, etc.? While the questions were being asked, people began to come in. Within five minutes every seat was taken. Young boys were seated in the window recesses, legs dangling. Adults crowded in at the back. Soon it was standing room only and the show began.

There is a fascination about films. People pay substantial prices for entrance into the movie theater and children sit transfixed in front of a television screen. Projected pictures attract attention. Those that move tend to hold attention because they are an ever-changing series of pictures that follow one after the other in rapid succession.

Teachers have learned that students respond with more interest when film-type media is used as a teaching aid. Therefore, the fully equipped media center is certain to have a variety of visual materials, such as filmstrips, slides, and even video cassettes. These, too, must be organized and made readily available for use. There are two schools of thought about how best to do this. Since both are "correct"

173

you will choose the one that works most satisfactorily with your congregation to encourage use of the material.

How you choose to shelve the material will depend upon how you expect it to be used. If you want to emphasize the multi-media approach to teaching, shelve all materials on a subject together where teachers and students can browse to make selections. In this case, all materials will be classified and assigned call numbers like the books.

If you want to conserve storage space and/or maintain maximum security for the materials, store the audio-visuals separately. When stored separately, most church libraries simply arrange these materials by their own unique accession number. However, Margaret Korty recommends an arrangement which is alphabetical by title (or subject followed by title). She finds this helps users to browse and find material without always having to check the card catalog.[1]

Take cataloging information from the title frame.

Motion Pictures

Motion pictures - sometimes referred to as "films" or "movies" - are a series of still pictures on film. When they are projected in rapid succession, they give the illusion of motion. Quite often they have a soundtrack that runs down one side of the film.

Motion pictures are described by the width of the film: 8, 16, 35, 55 or 70 millimeters. They come mounted on reels or in cartridges or cassettes. A film loop is a strip of film with the ends spliced together so the strip runs continuously. Usually a film loop is mounted in a cartridge.

Accessioning. Assign an accession number from a separate series of numbers beginning with the symbol "MP" or "motion picture." Example: "MP-1," "MP-2," etc. If the item is to be assigned a classification number like a book, type "MP" or "motion picture" above the call number. If it is to be filed by title (or subject and title) or accession number, use the symbol "MP" or the accession number as the call number.

Main entry. Since motion pictures are best known by their titles, enter under title. Take the title from the film itself, rather than from the container. After the title, include the designator "motion picture" in parentheses. For a film loop, use the more specific designator "motion picture loop." Add the name of the producer and the date of release. If the date of release is not known, use the copyright date if there is one.

Physical description. Essential elements of description are the running time (in minutes) and whether it is color or black-and-white film. However, preferred information includes the number of cartridges, cassettes or reels, the running time, whether the film is sound or silent, color or black-and-white, the width of the film (in millimeters) - in that order. Example: "2 reels. 52 min. sd. col. 16 mm." Type this information on the line below the date in the main entry, beginning at the second indention and continuing, if needed, with additional lines beginning at the first indention (see sample cards).

Notes. Maximum description on the catalog card is helpful in view of the fact that frequent handling of the film causes fingerprints and scratches. Enter information in the notes about accompanying material (if any), special equipment needed, unusual features (such as three-dimensional), age group of the intended audience, credits, and cast, brief summary of contents, and where filed (if not otherwise clear). For spacing, see sample cards.

If a film has been borrowed or rented - and probably will be borrowed again - make cards for the catalog. Flag it as a rental or loan item. Some libraries do this by entering the information on a different color card. Others underline the note: "Available on loan from [source]."

Type a set of catalog cards and a shelf-list card.

Marking. Inscribe the call number and the library's name on the film leader (if possible), the mount, and the container. A fine felt-tip pen writes quite satisfactorily on film. Stick-on labels designed to be used with motion pictures are available from standard library-supply sources.

Storing. Store the film in dustproof containers, away from the heat - preferably at 70°. Some libraries purchase film racks, which are designed to hold reels or cartridges and cassettes.

Sample Cards for Motion Pictures

```
call      Title....  (Motion picture)  (Card 2)
no
              Credits and cast.
              Summary or brief description of the
          content of the film.
```

```
call      Title....  (Motion picture)  Producer,
no.          date of release.

          number and format,  running time, sound
      or silent,  color or black & white,  width.

          Accompanying material, such as leader's
      guide.
          Age group of intended audience.
          Further physical description, such as
      special equipment required.

                              (Continued on next
                                   card)
```

Basic format

```
MP        The Holy Land.  (Motion picture)  Dr.
1             Marion S. Michael, 1975.

          1 reel, 10 min,  si,  color 8mm.

          Home movie taken by Dr. Michael on his
      trip to the Holy Land.  Features stations
      of the cross.
```

Main entry

Videotape Recordings

Videotape recordings contain program material designed for viewing on a television screen. They generally are identified by the width of the tape (1/4, 1/2, 3/4 or 1 inch), which is mounted on reels. Most often the reels are enclosed in a cartridge or cassette (a small cartridge). The cartridge may hold a single reel, two reels or a continuous loop. The single reel must be rewound to the beginning before the cartridge is disengaged from the machine. The two reel cartridge may be interrupted and the cartridge removed from the machine, but it does need to be rewound to the beginning to be shown again. The continuous loop does not need to be rewound. It can be interrupted and it will run continuously, repeating itself automatically.

Videotape recordings have a video signal and an audio signal. The video signal is described as color or black-and-white. The audio signal is identified by the number of tracks on the tape. For example, a two-track tape is monophonic sound, four-track is stereophonic, and eight-track is continuous-loop quadraphonic.

Accessioning. Assign an accession number from a series of numbers that begin with the symbol "VTR" or "videotape recording." Example: "VTR-1," "VTR-2," etc. If the item is to be classified, like a book, type the symbol "VTR" above the call number. If not, use just the symbol or the entire accession number as the call number.

Main entry. Enter under title. After the title include the designator "videotape recording" in parentheses. Add the name of the producer and date.

Physical description. Indicate the number of reels, whether cartridges or cassettes, running time, whether sound or silent, whether color or black-and-white, and width of tape. Example: "1 cassette. 60 min. sd. b&w. 3/4 in."

Notes. Enter information about accompanying material, such as leader's guide, special equipment needed (such as "for use with 3/4" U-Matic players"), unusual features, age group, credits and cast (if important), brief summary of contents, and where filed (if otherwise not obvious).

Type a set of catalog cards and a shelf-list card (see sample cards).

Marking. Inscribe the call number and the library's name on the mount and the container, if any. Stick-on labels work well and produce consistency in marking.

Storing. Like motion pictures, videotape recordings should be stored away from the heat, preferably at 70°.

Sample Cards for Videotape Recordings

```
call      Title.... (Videotape recording) Pro-
no.           ducer, date.

          number and format, running time, sound
          or silent, color or black & white, width.

          Special equipment needed.
          Suggested use.
          Age level.
          Brief summary of the contents of the
          videotape recording.
```

Basic format

Main entry for videotape recording

Slides

Slides are individual still pictures which, to be viewed, must be illuminated from the back or projected against a screen or light-colored wall. A standard slide is 35mm film mounted in a rigid cardboard or plastic frame which is 2" x 2" in size. It may be color or black-and-white. Related slides often are collected as a slideset. Some slide-sets have accompanying material, such as a reading script.

Special forms of slides require special equipment for showing. Examples are audioslides, lantern slides and stereoscopic slides. The audioslide has a strip of recorded sound attached to the side of the mount. The lantern slide is larger than a standard slide. The stereo-scope slide is composed of two identical slides mounted in a double frame; when projected, the picture becomes three-dimensional.

Accessioning. Assign an accession number preceded by the symbol "SL" or "slide." Example: "SL-1," "SL-2," etc. Use the symbol or the word "slide" above the call number if the slides are classified like books. Otherwise, use the symbol alone or with the accession number to indicate where it is filed.

Main entry. Enter under author or artist, if one is identified. Otherwise, enter under title. If the slide has no title, make one up and enter it in parentheses. Follow the title with the designation "slide" in parentheses, or the more specific designation "slideset," "audio-slide," "lantern slide" or "stereoscope slide." Include information about the editor, compiler, etc., if known and important. Add publisher and date.

Physical description. Indicate the number of slides, whether color or black-and-white, size of mount, and sometimes the type of container. If the slides are made of glass or some material other than film, write this word in parentheses after the number of slides. Example: "10 slides (glass)." Such slides often require special equipment to use. For stereoscopic slides, indicate the number of double frames or cards in the set. Example: "6 double fr." If other material is an integral part of the slide showing, such as a coordinated audio-recording (disc or cassette), add this information along with the recording's size and speed.

Notes. Enter information about accompanying material (such as a leader's guide), type of projector required (if not standard), age group of audience, brief summary of contents, and location (if not otherwise clear).

Type a set of catalog cards and a shelf-list card.

181

<u>Marking</u>. Label the call number and the library's name on the container. Letter the call number on the cardboard mount of each slide and number the slides in a set. Labels for slide mounts and boxes are available from library-supply houses.

<u>Storage</u>. Slides should be stored in boxes or arranged in trays or magazines ready for projection. Some libraries use manila or plastic envelopes. Slides should be protected from light and fingerprints and are best stored away from the dust and heat.

Sample Cards for Slides

```
call      Author or artist.
no.          Title..................... (Slide)
          Producer, date.

             number of frames, color or black & white,
          size, with audiorecording (disc or tape,
          sides or mounting, size, speed) and script
          (number pages)

             Age level.
             Summary.............................
```

```
          call      Title......................... (Slide)
          no.           Producer, date.

                         number of frames, color or black & white,
                      size in inches.

                         Leader's guide.
                         Special equipment needed.
                         Age level.
                         Summary................................
                      .....................
```

Basic card -
author or
artist,
main entry

Basic card - title main entry

182

```
SL      Easter.  (Slide)  Congregational Church,
81        1976.

        1 fr., color, 2 x 2 in.

        Summary:  Altar bedecked with lilies
        for the Easter Sunday worship service.
```

Single slide

```
        SL      Smeltzer, Wallace Guy.
                  The origins and early development of
                American Methodism.  (Slideset)  Author,
                c1962.

                  100 fr. (color, 2 x 2 in.), 1 record
                (12 in., 33-1/3 rpm), and manuscript.

                  Lecture consisting of slides coordinated
                with a phonograph record.
```

Slide set

```
SL      Daniel in the lion's den.  (Stereoscope
          slideset)  Concordia.

        3 cards (6 double fr.), color, 3-D.

        For use in Stori-viewer.
        Age group:  Pre-school and Primary.
```

Stereoscopic slide set

183

Transparencies

Transparencies, or vu-graphs, are similar to slides. They are much larger in size and generally are sheets of acetate film or some other transparent material. They may or may not have a cardboard frame. Transparencies are designed to be projected with an overhead projector. Since one can mark on them while they are being projected, they often substitute for a blackboard. Many are considered to be of temporary value.

Transparencies are easily created by hand lettering with colored felt-tip pens. If kept, they often are merely added to the vertical file. However, some are very carefully produced with the use of typewriters or graphic drawings. They may be mounted in cardboard frames. Some have overlays, which are one or more transparency sheets attached to one side of the frame and alter the original sheet when laid over it while it is being projected. These should be cataloged. A series of related transparency sheets may be collected and cataloged as a set.

Accessioning. Assign an accession number from a series of numbers that begin with the symbol "TRANS" or "transparency." Example: "TRANS-1," "TRANS-2," etc. If not cataloged like books, use this symbol or the entire accession number in place of the call number.

Main entry. Enter under title, if there is no author. If there is no title, make one up and enter it between parentheses. Add "transparency" in parentheses after the title. If it is a set, use the more specific designator "transparency set." Add the name of the producer and the date, if known.

Physical description. Indicate the number of sheets, whether color or black-and-white, and the size in inches. Even though overlays are attached to a transparency, it is still considered one piece.

Notes. Enter information about unusual features (such as overlays), age group, brief summary of contents or use, and location (if otherwise not clear - for example, transparencies not stored in envelopes sometimes are incorporated into the vertical file).

Type a set of catalog cards and a shelf-list card.

Marking. Label the transparency sheets and their container with the call number and the library's name. Number sheets in a set to keep them together. If there is no "title" sheet at the beginning of a set, make one - recording the same information you used as the main entry for cataloging.

Storing. Transparencies should be protected from light, fingerprints and dust. They are best stored in boxes or manila envelopes, away from the heat.

Sample Cards for Transparencies

```
call     Title.................... (Transparency)
no.         Producer, date.

            number of sheets, color or black & white,
         size in inches.

            Special features.
            Age level.
            Summary or use.....................
         ...............
```

Basic format

Main entry for transparency

Filmstrips

Filmstrips are unmounted rolls of 35mm film containing a series of related still pictures, which like slides are meant to be shown one at a time. Short filmstrips, often mounted in a rigid frame, are called filmslips (or viewstrips or stori-strips). If a filmstrip contains a soundtrack along one side of the film, or is accompanied by a synchronized record or cassette, it is called a sound filmstrip. Most filmstrips have accompanying material, such as a reading script, record or cassette.

If the accompanying material and the filmstrip are interdependent, the unit is cataloged as a filmstrip. If it can be used by itself, without the filmstrip, the unit should be cataloged as a kit (see chapter 11).

Accessioning. Assign an accession number from a series that begins with the symbol "FS" or "filmstrip." Example: "FS-1," "FS-2,"

186

etc. Some libraries use the symbol "SFS" for the sound filmstrips.
If the filmstrip is classified like a book, add the symbol or the
word "filmstrip" above the call number. If not, use the symbol or the
word "filmstrip," or the entire accession number in place of the call
number.

Main entry. Enter under title, unless an author is identified
on the title frame which precedes the main body of the filmstrip.
After the title, add the word "filmstrip" in parentheses - or the more
specific designator "filmslip" or "sound filmstrip." Add the name of
the producer and the date (if known).

Physical description. Indicate the number of frames, running
time (if known), sound (if a sound track is on the film), whether
color or black-and-white, and width of the film. If part of a series,
include the series name in parentheses. If more than one filmstrip is
cataloged as a single set, indicate the number of filmstrips rather
than the number of frames. If accompanying material is an integral
part of the showing, such as a record or tape cassette, add this with
the same descriptive information it would be given if cataloged
separately.

Notes. Add information that will help in using the filmstrip,
such as age group, any special equipment required and a summary of
contents.

Type a set of catalog cards and a shelf-list card.

Marking. Label the filmstrip itself and the container, as well as all accompanying material, with an indication of ownership and the call number. Use a fine felt-tip pen to label the leader strip of the film. On a filmslip, the label can be located on the frame, if there is one.

Storing. Like other film materials, filmstrips should be stored away from the heat and light and protected as much as possible from fingerprints and scratches. Boxes or drawers for storing filmstrip cans are available from the library supply houses.

Samples Cards for Filmstrips

```
call      Title................. (Filmstrip)
no.          Producer, date.

             number frames or filmstrips, color or
          black & white, width, and record (size,
          running time, speed)

             Notes.
```

Basic format

```
FS        Follow me; the story of the rich young
             ruler and the blind beggar. (Filmstrip)
          Alba House Communications, c1977.

          48 fr., color, 35 mm.

          Discussion guide and script.
          Suitable for children through adults and
          those with impaired hearing.
```

Main entry for filmstrip

```
FS        Jonah.  (Stori-strip)  Concordia.  R-43.

             20 fr., color, split/35 mm.  (Church-
          craft stori-strip series)

             Teacher's manual.
             Age group:  Children and Youth.
             Summary:  Background is included in the
          manual so that the Bible story can be seen
          in its setting of time.
```

Main entry for filmstrip (stori-strip)

```
SFS       Listen, I'll tell you a story.  (Sound
             filmstrip)  Graded press, c1977.

             64 fr., color, 35 mm, and 1 record (12 in.,
          20 min., 33-1/3 rpm)

             Script and guide.
             Age group:  Younger elementary.
             Summary:  Four stories from the Old
          Testament about Abraham and Sarah, Joseph,
          Moses and David.
```

Main entry for sound filmstrip

Microforms

Microforms contain filmed printed pages which have been so reduced in size that a viewing machine is necessary to read them. Forms include aperture cards, microfilm (reels, cartridges and cassettes), microfiche, ultrafiche, and micro-opaque cards (sometimes called microcards).

Aperture cards quite often are the size of keypunched cards and are distinguished by a small window of microfilm inserted, not always in the same place. Microfilm is a strip of film mounted on a reel, which may or may not be enclosed in a cartridge or cassette. Microfiche is one or more flat sheets of film with several rows of filmed pages on each sheet. Ultrafiche is like microfiche, but the images have been drastically reduced in size; for example, the entire Bible can be reproduced on one sheet of ultrafiche. Micro-opaque cards are a non-film type of microform.

Although most church and synagogue libraries are unlikely to have many microforms, they need to know how to handle them. They do save space and are relatively inexpensive to purchase. There are a few books that are available only in this format. Others might have a microfiche inserted in a pocket in the back. Back issues of many periodicals are available in microfilm or microfiche, which is an economical and space-saving way to store less frequently used material.

Accessioning. Assign an accession number beginning with a symbol that describes the microform, or the word itself. Symbols commonly used in libraries are "M" for microfilm and "MF" for microfiche. (Make sure you have not used "M" for maps or "MF" for map file.) Example: "MF-1," "MF-2," etc.

Use the call number you would assign to a bound copy with the word "microfilm" or "microfiche" above it (if filed with the books), the symbol or the word describing the medium (if filed by subject or title), or the accession number (if filed in accession number order).

Main entry. Use the same general rules that apply to cataloging the filmed material: if a book, enter under author (if any) and if a periodical, enter under title. Designate the medium in parentheses after the title. For example: "(Microfiche)." Add the name of the manufacturer or distributor of the microform. Date is optional.

Physical description. State the number of pieces (reels, sheets, cards or boxes of cards) and the size. For microfilm, give the width of the film in millimeters. For microfiche, micro-opaque cards and aperture cards, give the size of the sheets in inches. Examples:

(microfilm)   1 reel, 25mm.
(microfiche)   2 sheets, 4 x 6 in.
(micro-opaque) 3 cards, 3 x 5 in.

If the film is a negative film, say so; otherwise it is assumed to be positive.

Notes. Identify the publisher and date of the material, along with any other distinquishing features, in the notes.

Marking. Label everything. The call number and ownership mark should appear on all pieces. Use a fine felt-tip pen to mark directly on the film. Use pressure-sensitive labels on reels and containers.

Storing. Microfilm reels generally come in cardboard boxes. These can be stored on an open shelf or in a file drawer. Microfiche

191

and other microforms are best stored in a box or drawer. Some libraries place them in envelopes which are a little larger in size and can protect the film from dust whether they are filed away or being borrowed. All film should be kept away from heat and, as much as possible, be protected from fingerprints.

Examples of Catalog Cards for Microforms

Micro-   Wallace, Sarah Leslie.
film   Promotion ideas for public libraries.
          (Microfilm) University Microfilms Inter-
          national.

              1 reel, 35mm.

              Originally published by American Library
          Association, 1953. Illus.

Main entry - microfilm

MF   Jewish social studies. (Microfiche)
              Johnson Associates, Inc.

              Various sheets, 4 x 6 in.

              Periodical, quarterly.
              Library has
          v. 36, 1974
          v. 37, 1975
          v. 38, 1976

Main entry - microfiche

10/ Cataloging Sound Recordings

"How can we better reach out to our shut-ins, especially at this season?" The minister addressed his team of home visitors seated around the coffee table in his office. One of them was the church librarian who had been taking books (some of them in large print) to the shut-ins.

"They so miss coming to church," someone offered. "Maybe we could take them the recorded sermons."

"Their span of attention is so short," the minister mused thoughtfully.

The librarian spoke up. "Why don't we record a special tape, just for them - one that would run about ten or fifteen minutes? We could record it in the church chapel."

That struck a note. Someone else added, "We could begin and end with organ music." Another added, "Make it favorite hymns, they would like that." Warming to the idea, the minister added, "The message could be directed to them and be built around the special seasons."

That's how our tape service to shut-ins began. The church librarian, Dr. Stewart H. Webster, made all the arrangements, brought the recording equipment at the appointed time, and monitored the recording. He also cataloged the tapes for future use. In the beginning, the tapes were on reels that required rather bulky portable tape-playing equipment, but later were transfered to cassettes that could easily be flipped into a hand-held cassette player. This special service was received enthusiastically by the shut-ins as a personal message just for them.

Two types of audio recordings are most frequently found in libraries -- phonograph records (discs) and tape recordings (reels, cartridges and cassettes). They may contain musical or non-musical material. Some libraries describe these materials as phonodiscs or phonotapes. Others refer to them as audio recordings. However, in libraries where users must often look for materials without the help of a librarian, the terms records and tapes are used because they are more familiar.

Accessioning. Assign an accession number from a series that begins as follows:

> for records - R, _Rec_ or Record
>
> for open-reel-to-reel tapes - T, _TR_, RRT, Tape or Reel-
> to-reel tape.
>
> for reel tape mounted in cassettes - _TC_, Tape cassette,
> Cas, or Cassette
>
> for reel tape mounted in cartridges - _TC_, Tape cartridge,
> Car or Cartridge

Since audio recordings, video recordings and microforms come mounted on reels, cassettes and cartridges, I prefer the symbols which are underlined above. Also, some libraries like to identify record albums by using a separate accession number series that begins with "RA" (for record album), but this is not really necessary. Albums and single

194

records generally can be filed together, and the number of records in an album will be identified on the catalog cards.

Main entry. Enter in one of the following ways:

A single recording -- by composer or author, if known; otherwise by title

A collection -- by title, if there is one, or by the composer, author or title of the first piece recorded (the others can be listed in the notes)

If a performer (a person or group) is more significant than the material -- enter the recording under the name of the performer.

Since the title of music sometimes varies, use the more "popular" or a "uniform" title in parentheses ahead of the title identified on the recording. In this way all the recordings of the same music will file together. A uniform title is most often needed for classical music and is always constructed in the following order: form, medium of performance, number, opus, key. Example: "Concerto, piano, no. 5, op. 73, E flat." Follow the popular or uniform title with the medium designator in parentheses. If only the regular title is used, place the medium designator in parentheses after it. Add the distributor and his series number. Date is optional.

Physical description. Some church libraries find that the number of pieces (records, reels, etc.) and the playing time is enough information for the description. Even though simplified, standard library cataloging generally includes the number of pieces, the size, the speed and the recording mode. In general, the description should be complete enough to let the users know the kind of playing equipment that will be needed.

Records are described as follows:

Number of records or number of sides

Diameter of the record (7, 10 or 12 inches)

Recording speed (16-2/3, 33-1/3, 45 or 78)

Recording mode (monaural or stereophonic)

Playing time (in minutes) if known

Tapes are described as follows:

Tape reels (open-reel-to-reel tapes)

Number of reels

Size of reels (5 or 7 inches)

Playback speed (inches per second)

Recording mode (monaural or stereophonic)

Tape cassettes (reel-to-reel tapes in a casing)

Number of cassettes

Recording mode (monaural or stereophonic)

Tape cartridges (continuous-loop tapes in a casing)

Number of cartridges

Recording mode (monaural or stereophonic)

Most commercially available cassettes and cartridges are standard size and speed, so this information does not need to be included unless it is non-standard and would require special equipment. Monaural is two-track tape, and stereophonic is four-track or continuous-loop eight-track tape.

Notes. Give any important information about the format or use of the material that has not been included above (leader's guide, age group, credits, contents, etc.).

Marking. Label all pieces with the library name and the number that will identify the shelf location. Many libraries find the simplest method is to use the accession number as the call number.

Curved pressure-sensitive labels are available for records. A regular label can be used on the jacket. Attach a circulation card and pocket to the cardboard or paper jacket. If the record does not have one, it is wise to make one. Tape together three sides of two square pieces of paper which are a little larger than the record.

Although special labels are available for cassettes, the regular labels can be used - for tape reels, cartridges or cassettes - and also any boxes that might contain them. To attach the cover to a box that holds an open reel, affix a strip of Mystic tape along one side of the box when it is closed, so that the tape overlaps onto the bottom and top of the box. Open the cover and place a smaller piece of tape along the inside of the taped side to reinforce the hinge. The taped side will look like the spine of a book. Paste the circulation card and pocket inside the cover, unless the circulation cards for all audio-visual materials are to be filed in a circulation file. Some libraries use scheduling sheets instead of circulation cards.

Storing. Records should be handled by their edges and should not be stacked. They are best stored standing upright in protective covers

197

and away from the heat. Erwin John suggests storing single records in browser bins, face out to the user, with multiple-recording albums placed spine out on a shelf below the bins. [1]

Records should be cleaned from time to time with anti-static cloth. Mary Swicegood suggests they be washed with tepid water and a mild liquid detergent when badly soiled. Use a soft bristle brush to clean the grooves, rinse and drip dry. If a record still plays with surface noise after cleaning, play it wet. The water fills in the microscopic pits and acts as a cushion for the stylus. [2]

Tapes on open reels should be kept in their boxes. These can be lined up neatly on the shelf like books. Cassettes and cartridges are best filed in carousels, open trays or pull-out drawers. All tapes should be stored away from the heat and dust.

Examples of Catalog Cards for
Records and Tapes

```
Call    Author/composer name.
no.         Title.......... (Medium designator)  Manu-
        facturer/distributor, date.  Serial number.

        Number of pieces, size, speed, recording
        mode, playing time.

        Notes.
```

Basic format - Author/composer main entry

```
Call      Title............. (Medium designator)
no.         Manufacturer/distributor, date. Serial
            number.

            Number of pieces, size, speed, recording
          mode, playing time.

            Notes.
```

Basic format - Title main entry

```
Call      (Uniform title...............) (Medium
no.         designator)
          Regular title............. Manufacturer/
            distributor, date. Manufacturer's serial
            number.

            Number of pieces, size, speed, recording
          mode, playing time.

            Notes.
```

Uniform
title as
main entry

```
Call      Author/composer name.
no.          (Uniform title..........) (Medium desig-
          nator)
             Regular title............. Manufacturer/
            distributor, date. Serial number.

             Number of pieces, size, speed, recording
          mode, playing time.

             Notes.
```

Uniform title not as main entry

```
Rec      Jonathan Livingston Seagull.  (Record)
           ABC Records, 1973.  DSD-50160.

           2 sides, 12 in., 33-1/3 rpm, stereo.

           From the book by Richard Bach.
```

Record - Title main entry

```
Rec      Handel, George Frederick.
             (Messiah)  (Record)
             Handel's Messiah.  Somerset.  SF 15200.

             2 sides, 12 in., 33-1/3 rpm, stereo LP.

             Selections.
             London Philharmonic Choir with the London
           Philharmonic Orchestra, conducted by Walter
           Susskind.
             Summary:  Nine complete arias.
```

Record - Composer main entry, with popular title

```
TR        Booth, Edwin Prince.
            Martin Luther (Tape recording)  Bethesda
          Methodist Church, November 6, 1957.

            1 reel, 7 in., 7-1/2 ips, 45 min.

            Recorded by Gordon Linder.
            Christian Biography series.
```

Tape recording - Author main entry

```
TC        Repeat the sounding joy.  (Tape cassette)
            Graded press, 1973.

            1 cassette, 58 min.

            Leader's guide.
            Age group:  Elementary II-VI.
            For use with units dealing with the life
          and teachings of Jesus and Easter.  Six
          dramatic episodes run about 10 min. each.
```

Tape cassette - Title main entry

11/ Handling Other Media Materials

"Well, you can't say the library isn't used," a mother exclaimed as she watched three children happily sprawled out on a rug in the children's corner playing a game. The pieces were spread out on the rug. Quite clearly they felt at home. This library and the materials in it belonged to them. The librarian had been careful to arrange, mark and catalog the materials so that they were easy to locate and use.

A small media center is apt to have many non-book materials other than those previously described. These might include dioramas, games, kits, models, music and other items such as costumes, flannelgraphs, flash cards, flip charts, globes, puppets, toys and trophies.

The modern library handles all types of resource materials, including games.

Follow the same general cataloging rules that apply to other materials. Assign an accession number from a series that begins with the symbol that describes the type of material it is. Enter under author/creator if there is one, and under title if there is not. Follow the title with the medium designator in parentheses. Include source and date if known. Account for all major pieces in the physical description. Then, in the notes, explain unique features, how it might be used, and where it is filed. The basic card formats are as follows:

```
Call    Author/creator name.
no.         Title.............. (Medium designator)
        Source, date.

            Number of pieces, color, size, etc.
        (if more than 10 pieces use "various
        pieces)

            Age group.
            Summary..................................
        ..................
            Where filed.
```

Basic format - Author/creator main entry

```
Call      Title................  (Medium designator)
no.         Source, date.

            Number of pieces, color, size, etc.

            Leader's guide.
            How used.................
            Summary...............................
            ..................
```

Basic format - Title main entry

Dioramas

Dioramas are three-dimensional scenes in miniature. Usually they are a three-sided box with painted walls. The scene is constructed with miniature landscaping, objects, buildings and/or people.

Accession symbol: "Diorama."

Sample Card

```
Dio-      Going to church.  (Diorama)  Created by
rama        the fifth grade.  Concord Church, 1975.

            Various pieces, color, in box 36 x 24 x
          12 in.

            Contains model of church building, land-
          scaping, and people.
            Filed in library storage closet.
```

<u>Marking and storing</u>. Label the call number (accession number) and the library's name on the outside of the box. If possible, cover the box and store it on a shelf. Clear plastic is useful as a dust cover, because you can see what is inside.

Games

Games include puzzles and simulation games that teach or test concepts and behavior. Games usually have rules, equipment (such as a playing board) and pieces (such as cards, dice, spinning arrow, etc.)

If the game is mostly of written material, it may be added to the vertical file. Board games generally are cataloged separately.

<u>Accession symbol</u>: "G" or "Game."

Sample Cards

Game   The ungame. (Game) Ungame Co., c1975.

  1 game board with cards, dice and playing
pieces.

  For 2-6 persons to play.
  Age group: Children and Adults.
  Summary: Designed for each player to
experience the fun of learning to communicate more effectively.

. . . . .

```
Game    Benson, Dennis.
          Gaming; the fine art of creating simu-
        lation/learning games for religious edu-
        cation. (Simulation game) Abingdon,
        c1971.

        1 book and 2 records (8 in., 33-1/3 rpm)

        Incorporates the records as part of the
        text.
        Age group: Adult.

                            (Continued on next
                                  card)
```

```
Game    Benson, Dennis.
          Gaming....              (card 2)

        Summary: Eleven games are presented to
        show the potential gamesman how to design
        games to suit his particular need.
```

Marking and storing. Label ownership and call number on the box
and the major components (if possible). Some libraries list the contents
and paste the list inside the box top along with the circulation card
and pocket.

Reinforce the box edges with a strip of clear plastic or cloth tape. This helps them keep their shape. Their own weight tends to crush the boxes when they are stacked on a shelf or in a storage drawer. When they are stored on their edges, one beside the other, they are easier to take off and put back in place. However, you might need to make a Mystic tape hinge on one side of the cover or tie the box with string to keep the pieces together.

Kits

A kit is a collection of different types of media which may be used together or separately. They are packaged as a kit because they all relate to the same specific subject. A kit may contain filmstrips, booklets, flash cards, records, etc. They are cataloged as a unit when they have greater potential as a kit than if cataloged separately.

<u>Accession symbol</u>: "K" or "Kit."

Sample Card

```
Kit     Move when the spirit says move.  (Kit)
           Graded press, c1976.

           2 filmstrips (14 fr. ea., color), 1 record
        (12 in., 33-1/3 rpm), and 10 cards

        Leader's guide and script.
        Age group:  Middle elementary.
        Summary:  Helps students and teachers
     learn basic movements for creative inter-
     pretation of biblical stories, hymns, and
     seasons.
```

Marking and storing. Somewhere in the kit, include a list of the pieces. Label the call number and the library's name on each major piece. Store in the original carton if possible.

Models and Realia

Models are representations. Realia are the real thing. Handicraft items might be one or the other. For example, models include such things as scale models of buildings, miniature scrolls, or papier-mâché animals. Realia are actual paper scrolls, earthenware jars, costumes, trophies, etc.

Accession symbols: "Mod" or "Model" and "Realia."

Sample Cards

```
Model    India woman doll.  (Model)  SERRV. #36903.

         1 doll, 11 in. high.

         This model demonstrates the traditional
         sari costume of India.
         Filed in library storage closet on a
         shelf for costumed dolls.
```

Marking and storing. Store in a box, if possible. Label the box
as well as the bottom of the object with the call number (accession
number) and the library's name. Store in a drawer reserved for this
purpose, or on a shelf in a closet.

Music

Musical scores are printed material and therefore are cataloged
in much the same way as books.

Accession symbol: "MS," "Music" or "Musical score."

Several copies of a single anthem are treated as a set. The set
is given one accession number and each copy within the set is assigned a
copy number.

Main entry. Enter under composer, if known, and under title if not.
Popular titles or uniform titles are used when necessary to keep the
various versions of the same music together in the card catalog. (See
discussion of uniform titles under sound-type recordings.) The musical

forms that generally do require a uniform title are cantatas, chorales, concertos, duets, masses, motets, operas, overtures, sonatas, symphonies, etc.

Many church librarians find it useful to have an added entry under: (a) title; (b) event of the liturgical year, such as Advent, Christmas, Epiphany, etc.; (c) Biblical reference, if there is one, such as OLD TESTAMENT - GENESIS, etc.; (d) HYMNS, if it also is in the church hymnal; and (e) subject topics such as PRAISE, PRAYER, etc. Quite often a separate card catalog is maintained in the choir room, and sometimes the scores are filed there as well.

<u>Marking and storing</u>. Even when they are not assigned a classification number, music scores are stamped and labeled like books. If not classified like books, use the accession number as the call number. Add the copy number below the call number. Example:
```
MS
378
c.16
```
Store in pamphlet boxes on the shelf.

Sample Cards

```
MS       Adam, Adolphe.
            Oh, holy night; cantique de noël.
         (Musical score)  G. Schirmer, c1935.

            For voice and piano.
            Key of C.
```

Musical score - Author main entry

```
MS        (Oh, come all ye faithful) (Musical
          score)
          Concertato on Adestes Fideles, with organ
          and brass.  Augsburg Publishing House,
          c1976.

          Key of D.
          Arranged by Austin C. Lovelace.
```

Musical score - Popular title main entry

Other Media

Flannelgraphs are figures used on a flannel board. The flannel
board is covered with material to which the suitably backed cutout
figures will adhere when pressed firmly against it. The boards are
treated as equipment unless they are kept together with the flannelgraph
materials. In most libraries these materials are kept in the vertical
file, under subject.

Flash cards are uniform-size cards in a set. Usually they have
printed numbers, letters or pictures which are meant for rapid showing
as in a test or drill. These, too, are treated as vertical-file material.

Flip charts usually are composed of large sheets of paper fastened
together at the top so they can be flipped over the top of a stand. They
are meant for viewing one at a time before a group of people. They are
cataloged, if at all, like maps and other charts.

Globes are cataloged like models. Include the same information
you would for maps and add the diameter of the globe in the physical
description. Globes that have raised surfaces to indicate relative
heights of mountains and valleys are described as relief globes.

Archives are made up of official records of membership, weddings,
baptisms and deaths. They also are an accumulation of social history
such as worship bulletins, newsletters, scrapbooks, photographs, programs
for special events, etc. These are materials historians will want
to look at. They are evidence of how various groups made their decisions
over the year. Usually they do not circulate, and more than likely they
will not be described in the card catalog. Since they require special
handling, they should be identified and stored under the guidance of a
person or committee entrusted with their care.

12/ Encouraging Use of the Catalog

"How do I get people to use the catalog?"

This question has been asked me more than once. Recently, a friend wrote, "I put many hours in on cataloging and classifying and typing, and when I see people 'browsing' instead of using the catalog I get somewhat annoyed." She asked for suggestions about use of the card catalog, why it isn't used more, how to make it more effective, etc.[1]

In part, my reply was as follows: "From my own experience I find that some people prefer to browse unless searching for a specific title, author, series, etc., or books on a topic more specific than the general classification categories. Perhaps holding sessions with the teachers to show them how to use it effectively or listing the topics in it which relate to their teaching curriculum would help. As for the average library user, if they ask me about a certain book or topic, I generally take them to the card catalog (even if I know where to find it on the shelf) and we go through the search steps together. Hopefully, the next time they will search for themselves."

Showing the Way

Someone once said that libraries are organized for librarians. We need to correct this impression. We need to organize the catalog for the users and then show them how it really is their helper.

To do this, provide written material and visual aids - road signs, so to speak - that help to explain the arrangement of materials, the classification scheme and the index to the collection (the catalog).

PLEASE DON'T FORGET

① CARD CATALOG LISTS BOOKS BY AUTHOR, TITLE AND SUBJECT

② FICTION IS SHELVED BY AUTHOR, NON-FICTION BY CALL NUMBER

③ ASK THE LIBRARIAN IF YOU NEED ASSISTANCE

Signs. Post attractive, easy-to-read signs, with print large enough to read, as follows:

Near shelving: Post a sign that explains the overall classification scheme. Posters that explain the Dewey Decimal system are available from most of the library-supply houses.

On each section of the shelving: Label the general collection, such as Fiction, Non-fiction, Reference, etc.

On each shelf: Label the topics, such as BIBLE, CHILD STUDY, RELIGIOUS EDUCATION, etc. Movable metal label holders that slip on the shelves are available from most library-supply houses.

On the card catalog (or nearby): Post a sign that tells what the catalog contains and how it is arranged.

Somewhere in the library (or outside): Post a sign to remind people that you have a catalog and, if its location is not obvious, tell where it is located.

Lettering - by its size, style and background - attracts attention. Signs large and clear enough will lead a reader more quickly to his field of interest. Many arts-and-crafts books give instructions on how to make various types of letters, including three-dimensional effects. John Hack gives the following advice: "Letters must be large enough to be read and in adequate contrast to the background....As a general rule, the simpler the style the easier the visual will be to read. All capital, block letters in simple 'comic-strip' style are recommended as the most reada- ble. (The letters are also the easiest for the amateur to prepare.)" He describes various types of lettering, which include typewriter type, magnetic letters and symbols, cling-type letters, hook-and-loop materi- als, pin-back letters, die-cut letters, dry transfer lettering, rubber stamps, stencils and templates, as well as freehand lettering. "Perhaps the simplest visual (other than the chalkboard) is made by writing on a newspaper want ad page with a shoe polish dauber. It makes a surprising- ly attractive and readable visual."[2] Try this for your next display of new books.

Catchy titles attract attention, too. Try popular phrases to iden- tify those special shelves for study classes. Go back to your reference file of language the congregation uses. Pick out familiar phrases.

Take advantage of current fads or interests. Change the signs from time
to time. Look in publishers' catalogs and curriculum guides for ideas.
Scan book titles, too. The following were gleaned from these sources:

Roots of Our Heritage	God's Hotline
Meditation and Relaxation	Fighting Adversity
Leadership in Action	The Good News
Teaching Kids	Status of Women
Gospel Characters	Death and Difficult Days
Power-packed Stories	Emerging Missions
Evangelical Outreach	Jobs and Careers
Spiritual Insights	Paul's World
The Biblical Approach	

Instructional cards. Place cards in the catalog itself that explain what the catalog contains and how it is arranged.

At the beginning of the file: Include a card that indicates the
type of materials included (such as books only, or books and non-book
materials), the arrangement (such as one alphabet like a dictionary, or
separate alphabets for authors, titles and subjects) and the abbreviations used on the cards (such as "ed." for editor and edition). "How
to Use this Catalog," guide cards printed on heavy card stock with tabs
reinforced with plastic, are available from Gaylord Brothers as well as
the other supply houses. They come as a package of ten, so one can be
placed in the front of each catalog drawer.

At the beginning of a major subject heading: Type a card which
explains what the subject does or does not cover.

216

Throughout the catalog: Make liberal use of cross-reference cards to lead the user to a specific subject term used or to other related material.

In the notes on a catalog card: Indicate where the material is filed, if other than the regular shelf arrangement. This applies to special shelf locations, such as reference and oversize collections. (Some libraries prefer to use a small stamp over the call number to indicate special locations.) This also applies to non-book materials which, because of size or packaging, requires them to be filed in closets, pull-out drawers or special cabinets.

Booklets. Issue a booklet about the library and its services, and include a section on the shelf arrangement, the classification scheme and the card catalog. For example, St. Matthew's United Methodist Church Houston, Texas, issued a booklet which included a section on "The Card Catalog" which reads as follows:

> The card catalog is an alphabetical file on all books
> in the library. Each book is listed by author, title, and/
> or subject, in one alphabetical arrangement. There is a
> Card Catalog for Adults, Youth, Juniors, and Children.

> If you'd like to know whether we have THE ROBE by
> Lloyd C. Douglas, look in the drawer labeled to include
> "R" (disregard A, An, The, when it is the first word of
> a title) and you will find it listed in its alphabetical
> place, and the call number or letter in the upper left

corner shows where the book is located on the shelf.   In
this case, THE ROBE would be F   or Fiction.[3]
                              Dou

Bookmarks. The Children's Book Council, Inc. (175 Fifth Avenue,
New York, NY 10010) has a printed bookmark which describes, attractively and simply, the ten main subject groups in the Dewey Decimal Classification scheme. Sturgis Library Products (Box 130, Sturgis, MI 49091)
offers a similar bookmark decorated with angels. Some libraries print
(or mimeograph, color and cut out) their own bookmarks to explain the
simple rules for use on one side and to outline the classification
scheme on the other. Bookmarks are useful as handouts, or they may be
distributed with a morning worship bulletin.

Displays. Try featuring the card catalog in one of the library's
displays. The students of Cardinal McClosky High School (Slingerland,
New York) painted murals on the school library's walls to explain graph-
ically the Dewey Decimal Classification. Each of the ten hundreds
classes was illustrated by a caveman pondering such questions as "Who
is the man in the next cave?" (300s), and "What makes things happen in
the world around me?" (500s).[4]

Feature articles. Write a column for the church paper to explain
what the library has, how it is arranged and how the catalog can help
the parishioners use the collection. Make it light-hearted and inte-
resting. Perhaps include a story about the minister and his wife using
it successfully.

Procedures manual. Allow the library's cataloging procedures to be

218

available to the users as well as to the workers. Let them see in
greater detail just how the materials are handled, if they wish to
pursue this.

<h3 style="text-align:center">Teaching Users</h3>

Use every opportunity to instruct library users, if they do not
already know, about the arrangement of materials and how to use the
catalog.

Teach all ages how they can help themselves by using the catalog.

Demonstrate use. I find that some people prefer to be left alone
to browse. Others, especially those searching for a specific title,
author, etc., might ask for help. When they do, I generally take them
to the card catalog (even if I know where to find it on the shelf) and
we go through the search steps together. Hopefully, the next time they
will search for themselves.

<u>Visit classrooms</u>. Take the initiative with church school leaders. Approach the director of religious education and the department heads. Go armed with curriculum guides. Be prepared to show how they might tie in use of the catalog with what the classes are studying. Create enthusiasm for what the library can do for them in teaching. When teachers become skilled in using the library, they introduce it quite naturally to their students when the need arises. Offer to visit the classes to explain use of the catalog and what can be found through its use.

<u>Class visits to library</u>. Coordinate with the teachers to schedule class visits to the library. Demonstrate the arrangement of materials and use of the catalog. Let the students test their ability to use it themselves. Young people are very effective teachers of each other, so try dividing the class into pairs. Give each pair a drawer from the catalog and ask them to locate answers to a list of simple questions.

<u>Games</u>. It's fun to learn through games. Use games that teach library skills. For example, Shari Wallace, an elementary-school librarian, developed an inexpensive, elementary-level card game to teach library skills. Cards depict major Dewey classifications as well as many of the subdivisions to demonstrate the relationship between book subjects and Dewey numbers. The game, called "Shelve-It," now is available from the Highsmith Company (Box 25, Fort Atkinson, WI 53538). It can be used in three ways: as flash cards, as a search game for primary grades, and as a card game for two to six players in grades 3 to 6.[5]

A "mini-catalog" method of testing a new student's familiarity with the catalog was developed at the Middleville Junior High School (Northport, New York). It consists of two parts: an individual card catalog and a test based on this catalog. The "individual" card catalog was made up from catalog cards that had been withdrawn from the library's regular card catalog. These cards were duplicated to make several individual or "mini-catalogs" with author, title and subject sections. Plastic spirals held them together. The test was comprised of fifteen questions structured on a simple location basis. For example: "Give the title of a book by _____"; "What is the call number of a book on the subject of _____." Questions that arose during the taking of the test served to pinpoint individual weaknesses as well as any confusion that existed. This is something that can be done in a classroom.[6]

The same approach was used in a learn-by-doing program to develop the "library habit" in children living in rural areas where over seventy percent of the adult population is functionally illiterate. A small card catalog, books grouped by subject area, lists of questions, and other instructional aids were taken to schools in each county eight times over a period of six months. The students gradually were taught how to locate books on the library shelves, how to use subject, author and title entries in a card catalog, how to understand a very generalized and simple version of the Dewey Decimal system and how to use cross references in a card catalog, among other things. Then the students were taken on an extensive tour of the library and issued library cards. The children liked the program and voluntarily participated without the offer of rewards such as gold stars or school grades.[7]

Puzzles were used in another experiment. "I had been making puzzles from book jackets for some time," Maxime Cornwell reported, "and, realizing that these were more popular than books with some children, I developed the idea of using these puzzles to teach library skills. They have proven to be highly successful tools...to encourage students to use the catalog." She uses mat board, paint, and rubber cement (on both the board and the jacket before pasting) and lets it dry overnight. A paper cutter trims the edges and cuts vertical strips between 1" and 2" in width. These strips then are cut into straight or slanted pieces that vary in size from 1½" to 3", taking care to make sure that a part of a figure, letter or color shows on either side of a cut. All the pieces are filed in a labeled manila envelope. Younger players are asked to assemble the puzzle and then find the first letter of the author's name on the puzzle, then on the puzzle envelope, and finally to look for the book on the shelf. Older children are asked to look for more information and to check the card catalog for shelf location.[8]

Coloring books. Some libraries compile coloring books to help teach younger children about the library. "Color Me Carnegie," a coloring book distributed by the Moscow Public Library (Moscow, Idaho), includes an introduction to the card catalog. One double-page spread reads (in fat colorable letters and pictures): "All of the things you can check out of the Library are listed in THE CARD CATALOG which is - Guarded by 'Groshanka' and 'Sofi' the Gerbils."

Puppet shows. Try writing a script for puppets. This will hold the attention of adults as well as children to get across the story of the card catalog. Over 250 different kinds of mitt-type puppets can be obtained from the Puppet Tree Company (Box 63, Berwyn, PA 19312). The variety of puppets includes people, clothing, birds, animals, insects, plants, etc., and all are washable.

The Minneapolis Public Library's Roosevelt Branch made a puppet that was a "talking" book catalog to instruct youngsters in the use of the library. A tape-recorder script accompanied the puppet show. A take-home cartoon sheet reinforced what the children learned during the program.[9]

Ask your public library for suggested sources of other instructional materials, such as films, filmstrips and books, for teaching use of the library.

Nurturing the Collection (and the Catalog)

"The content of our faith is changeless, but the form of our faith must change with every age," said Dr. James Logan, Professor of Systematic Theology. "If we are out of time, what we present is apt to be out of time."[10] He was speaking about libraries. One must remain alert to changing needs of the congregation. Then, one must be flexible enough to allow an established system to be changed in order to respond.

In regard to change, Esther Piercy offers a word of caution: "Although it is foolish to continue bad practices...it is also unwise to assume immediately that all the past is bad and begin something one cannot finish or something which will keep the catalog in a turmoil for a long time." Her advice is to decide why things were done as they were, what will be gained by a change and what is the best way to effect the change. Adopt shortcuts, such as writing in new subject headings above old ones and leaving the cards in file to be retyped later. Use cross references to tie the old and the new headings together.[11]

Keep current. Each year when you review the needs of the congregation, review the content and appearance of the collection - and the card catalog.

"Don't be afraid to discard books!" says Juanita Carpenter. "Old books are self-defeating. If there are titles among them that you want for the library, buy new copies. It is so very important that you open your church library with shelves of attractive books that invite browsing and reading."[12]

When material has not been taken out for a year or two, it should be taken off the shelf and withdrawn from the collection. Make room for material more in demand. Reference books are the exception. Generally, they will be kept as long as their content is pertinent and contemporary.

Keep the catalog up to date, too. When books and other materials are withdrawn, promptly mark or pull the cards, as follows:

Shelf-list card: Draw a line through the accession number of the withdrawn book. Stamp or write "withdrawn" and the date to show when it was taken out of the collection. If there are other copies still in the collection, leave the shelf-list card in file. If there are no

224

other copies in the collection, pull the shelf-list card from the file. Some libraries keep the pulled cards in a separate "withdrawn" file. Others simply discard them.

Catalog cards: If there are other copies in the collection, leave all the catalog cards in file. If there are no other copies, remove all the catalog cards. (This is when you will appreciate the tracing on the back of the main card, so you can find all the cards that were filed in the catalog.)

Remove the call-number label, if possible, and mark "withdrawn" across the ownership stamp. Remove the circulation card and pocket. Dispose of withdrawn material by giving it away, or contribute it to the congregation's next used-book sale.

Be innovative. When new material is added on topics not previously in the collection, consider again the uniqueness of your congregation. How will your people look for it when they come to the library? People of a community tend to develop a language of their own - idioms, familiar phrases, etc. - that do not mean the same thing to other communities or other parts of the country. Involve the users in developing new subject terms. Don't be afraid to use topics different from those used by the Library of Congress or other processing services.

Be consistent. Make sure you have a grounding in good basics before you improvise and your catalog will evolve with a logic that someone else can follow. This is important for the searcher. Once he has learned the "key" to what you have done, he should be able to apply it to find a specific book, picture, or filmstrip, or to locate general categories of material through which he can browse.

Keep in mind that you are creating more than just a record of materials. You are helping people find the material they need.

Be enthusiastic. Present the catalog with enthusiasm. Don't apologize for its shortcomings. Make it as neat as possible. Have clean, legible labels and guide cards. Retype rather than file cards with typos. Provide clear, simple instructions for use.

Let the catalog convince each parishioner that you have a collection of books and other materials that he needs and wants - to enrich his spiritual life, to increase his knowledge and understanding of the Bible, to help him lead his family in the way of the faith, and to prepare him for his work in the congregation. Let it identify easily where specific items are shelved - as a road map to the collection. Reinforce the catalog by posting directional signs and shelf markers, teaching use of the catalog, and involving others in its development and nurture. That's what cataloging is all about.

Notes

Chapter 2

1. Personal letter dated April 16, 1964.

2. "A Pre-School Child's Visit to the Library" by Violet M. Neger. Church and Synagogue Libraries, vol. 8, January-February 1975, pp. 1, 12.

3. Dotts, Maryann J., The Church Resource Library: How to Start and Make It Grow. Nashville, TN: Abingdon Press, 1976, p. 18.

4. "Operating a Church Library" by Mrs. Sidney W. Clark. The Bethany Preview, Fall 1965, pp. 11-12.

5. "How to Classify Books in the Church Library" by Irene Davis. Bethany Preview, Spring 1965, p. 17.

6. Piercy, Esther J., Commonsense Cataloging. Bronx, NY: H. W. Wilson Co., 1965, p. 67.

7. Weine, Mae, Weine Classification Scheme for Judaica Libraries, 6th ed., 1975. Distributed by Synagogue, School, and Center Division, Association of Jewish Libraries, c/o Dr. Leonard Gold, Jewish Division, New York Public Library, New York, NY 10018. (The companion volume is Relative Index to the Weine Classification Scheme for Judaica Libraries by Anita Loeb, 1972.)

8. "St. Pius X Library, Shrine of the Most Blessed Sacrament, Washington, D. C." by Sylvia Cox. Church and Synagogue Libraries, vol. 3,

November 1969, pp. 3-4.

9. "The Church Library Aids the Parish Program" by Edith Maxfield.
The Christian Educator, vol. 9, July-September 1966, pp. 3-4, 29.

10. "Classification and Cataloging in a Parish Library" by Joyce L.
White. Catholic Library World, vol. 48, May-June 1977, pp. 428-30.

11. "Color Me Young and International" by Janie Filstrup. Wilson Library
Bulletin, vol. 50, October 1975, pp. 161-65.

12. Piercy, Esther J., Commonsense Cataloging. Bronx, NY: H. W. Wilson
Co., 1965, p. 24.

Chapter 3

1. "Classification and Cataloging in a Parish Library" by Joyce L. White. Catholic Library World, vol. 48, May-June 1977, pp. 428-30.

2. "Washington Hebrew Congregation, Washington, D. C." by Alice F. Toomey. Church and Synagogue Libraries, vol. 3, January 1970, pp. 11-12.

3. "A Library Serves the Whole Church" by Erwin E. John. International Journal of Religious Education, vol. 38, October 1961, pp. 15-16.

4. "Book Classification is Essential to Library Usefulness" by Gertrude Ackermann Ogden. Lutheran Libraries, vol. 6, Summer 1964, p. 6.

5. Letter to Cowman Publishing Company, Los Angeles, dated February 4, 1964.

6. "The Library First Lutheran Church, Ellicott City, Maryland" by Mrs. Herbert M. Payne. Church and Synogogue Libraries, vol. 3, May 1970, p. 7.

7. "Reading is What is Happening" by Sabrina Porter. Church and Synagogue Libraries, vol. 3, July 1970, pp. 9-11.

8. "Open Every Day, Church Library Multiplies its Metropolitan Ministry" by Charlotte Allen. Church and Synagogue Libraries, vol. 10, July-August 1977, pp. 1, 7.

9. Dotts, Maryann J., The Church Resource Library; How to Start It and Make It Grow. Nashville, TN: Abingdon Press, 1976, p. 17.

10. "On the Frontier," <u>Church and Synagogue Libraries</u>, vol. 3, May 1970, p. 5.

11. Smith, Ruth S., <u>Cataloging Books Step by Step</u>. Bryn Mawr, PA: Church and Synagogue Library Association, 1977, p. 10.

Chapter 4

1. Buder, Christine, <u>How to Build a Church Library</u>. St. Louis, MO: Bethany Press, 1955, p. 17.

2. Celnik, Max, <u>The Synagogue Library: Organization, Administration</u>. New York: Library Services Bureau, The United Synagogue of America, 1967, p. 4.

3. "Pooling Ideas" by Audrey Mueller. <u>Lutheran Libraries</u>, vol. 6, Spring 1964, p. 9.

Chapter 5

1. Letter from Rachel Kohl, dated September 21, 1977.

2. "Library Offers Way to Cope with Mildew, Mold on Books." <u>Gaylord's Triangle</u>, vol. 44, September 1964, p. 2.

Chapter 6

1. "Betty Bookworm" by Betty Lou Hammargren. <u>Church and Synagogue Libraries</u>, vol. 4, January 1971, p. 7.

2. "Before You Grab Your Dewey!" by Jacqulyn Anderson. <u>Media; Library Services Journal</u>, vol. 2, July-August-September 1972, p. 24.

3. "Prime Marks in Library of Congress Notation" by Juanita Carpenter. <u>Lutheran Libraries</u>, vol. 16, Summer 1974, p. 59.

4. "Subject Headings Trauma; Making Do With First Aid" by Dorothy Kanwischer. <u>Wilson Library Bulletin</u>, vol. 49, May 1973, pp. 651-54.

5. "Analytic Cards Improve Card Catalog" by Juanita Carpenter. <u>Lutheran Libraries</u>, vol. 13, Winter 1970, p. 5.

6. Letter from Rachel Kohl, Chairman, Library Services Committee, Church and Synagogue Library Association, dated September 21, 1977.

7. "Tell Me, Please" by Marilyn Hager. <u>Church Library Magazine</u>, vol. 7, June 1966, p. 11.

8. Nickel, Mildred L., <u>Steps to Service; a Handbook of Procedures for the School Library Media Center</u>. Chicago: American Library Association, 1975, p. 54.

9. "Modifying Printed Cards" by Bernard Polishuk. <u>School Library Journal</u>, vol. 21, April 1975, p. 35.

Chapter 8

1. "The Care and Filing of Pictures" by Imo Ruyle Foster. <u>International</u> <u>Journal of Religious Education</u>, vol. 40, September 1963, pp. 14-16.

2. "A Library Serves the Whole Church" by Erwin E. John. <u>International</u> <u>Journal of Religious Education</u>, vol. 38, October 1961, pp. 15-17.

3. "Banners are Like Libraries" by Rose Mary Ulland. <u>Church and Syna-</u> <u>gogue Libraries</u>, vol. 6, November-December 1972, pp. 9, 11.

Chapter 9

1. Korty, Margaret Barton, <u>Audio-visual Materials in the Church Library</u>; <u>How to Select, Catalog, Process, Store, Circulate, and Promote</u>. River-dale, MD: Church Library Council, 1977, p. 11.

Chapter 10

1. "Organization of Audio-Visuals and Non-Book Materials in a Church Library" by Erwin John. <u>Lutheran Libraries</u>, vol. 19, Spring 1977, p. 37.

2. Talk on "Care of Library Materials" by Mary Swicegood, at the Seventh Annual Church Library Workshop, Washington, D.C., April 15, 1967, sponsored by the Church Library Council.

Chapter 12

1. Letter from Cynthia M. Stansfield, Manchester, CT, undated.

2. Hack, John, How to Make Audiovisuals. Nashville, TN: Convention Press, 1973, pp. 23-36.

3. St. Matthew's United Methodist Church Library. Houston, TX, St. Matthew's United Methodist Chruch, no date, p. 5.

4. "Classification Information." Wilson Library Bulletin, vol. 49, October 1974, p. 131.

5. "Buyer's Guide" by Thomas W. McConkey. Library Journal, vol. 103, January 1, 1978, p. 83.

6. "Card Catalog Teaching Aid" by Sylvia Heitert. School Library Journal, vol. 98, September 15, 1973, p. 44.

7. "Project Uplift: Cultivating the Library Habit" by John L. Shelton. Wilson Library Bulletin, vol. 50, September 1975, pp. 59-62.

8. "Puzzle Catalog" by Maxine Cornwell. Library Journal, vol. 99, April 15, 1974, p. 1203.

9. "Library Display." Wilson Library Bulletin, vol. 49, November 1974, p. 214.

10. "Dr. Logan Speaks on the Role of Libraries." News Bulletin (Church and Synagogue Library Association), vol. 1, Winter 1967, p. 2.

11. Piercy, Esther J., <u>Commonsense Cataloging: A Manual for the Organization of Books and Other Materials in School and Small Public Libraries</u>. New York: H. W. Wilson Company, 1965, p. 15.

12. "Libraries Need Weeding and Feeding" by Juanita Carpenter. <u>Lutheran Libraries</u>, vol. 17, Summer 1975, p. 55.

Appendix

Accessioning: The process of recording new additions to the collection in a record book, as property. The record book is called an
accession book. The items are numbered in sequence as they are entered
into the book and these are the accession numbers.

Added entry: A card in the catalog which is a copy of the main
card with additional information, such as title, joint author's name
or subject, inserted at the top. The information added at the top
makes the card file alphabetically in another location in the catalog.

Analytic entry: A card in the catalog for a part of a book, such
as a short story or poem in a collection, or a chapter or part of a
chapter not covered by a subject heading and of sufficient importance
to identify in the catalog. The analytic entry also is an added entry.

Annotation: A brief description or review of the contents of a
book or other media item.

Anonymous: Without a name, such as a book with no identified author. Stories which have passed down from generation to generation often have no author and these are called anonymous classics.

Author entry: A card in the catalog with the author's name as the
top line. Usually the author entry is the main entry.

Author symbol: One or more letters of the author's last name or the first letter and numbers that represent the name. The author symbol is added below the classification number to form a call number.

Authority file: A record of names, subject headings or abbreviations as they are to be used in the catalog, to assure consistency in cataloging. For example, a subject-heading list is an authority file, whether you compile your own or use one someone else has published.

Bibliography: A list of references to library-type material which identifies author, title, place, publisher, date and sometimes pages.

Book card: The circulation card which generally is inserted in a book pocket pasted inside the back cover. This card is used to record the date of circulation and the name of the borrower.

Book selection: The process of choosing books to be added to a library collection.

Building a catalog: The process of preparing cards that describe library materials and interfiling them in a catalog according to a pre-designed plan. The catalog is "built" as more and more cards are filed into it.

Call number: A number which identifies a specific shelf location for a book or other item. Usually it is made up of a subject classification number and an author symbol.

Card set: All the cards that describe one book or other media item. A card set consists of the main-entry card and all added entries, which are listed in the tracing.

Classification number: A number that represents a subject.

Classifying: The process of determining the subject of a book or other item and assigning a classification number or subject heading to represent the subject.

Copyright: A protection granted by law against unauthorized copying of an original work which has been registered with the U.S. Copyright Office. The copyright date is the date that the copyright was granted by the government and usually appears on the back of the title page.

Entry: The first line on a catalog card. The entry determines where the card will be filed in the catalog.

Guide card: A card in the catalog with a labeled tab that stands above the other cards to indicate the alphabetical cards that follow it. A guide card might show a letter of the alphabet or a subject. In the shelf-list file, the guide cards indicate numbers.

Holdings: What the library has (or holds) in the collection.

Imprint: The place of publication, publisher's name and date of publication is called the imprint. Usually, the publisher's name and location are printed on the title page. The date most often is on the back of the title page.

<u>Indention</u>: The number of typewriter spaces from the left edge of the card where the typing begins. For example, the <u>first indention</u> might be nine spaces, the <u>second indention</u> eleven spaces, and the <u>third indention</u> thirteen spaces.

<u>Index</u>: A detailed listing of topics covered in the book, usually arranged alphabetically with references to pages in the book.

<u>Jacket</u>: A paper cover folded around a new book's cover to protect it from dust and handling. The attractive color, printing and design of a jacket often help to promote sale of the book as well.

<u>Jacket blurb</u>: A brief description or review of a book and/or the author's background, printed usually on the inside flaps or on the back of a dust jacket.

<u>Main entry</u>: The first line of information on the main card, or the basic card from which all others are copied.

<u>Medium designator</u>: A word or words used to describe non-books. For example: filmstrip, record, game, kit, etc.

<u>Open entry</u>: A card in the catalog that provides a place for new issues and volumes to be added as they are received.

<u>Prime mark</u>: A mark like an apostrophe; used by the Library of Congress to indicate where a Dewey Decimal number should be cut to make it shorter and simpler.

Reprint: A republication of a book in facsimile, or with very minor changes such as correction of typographical errors; not a new edition.

Revised edition: A new edition; a new printing of a book with major changes, such as rewritten sections, addition of material, new illustrations, or a changed title.

"See also" reference: A direction card in the catalog that refers from a name or subject heading that is used to another related one, from something to something more.

"See" reference: A direction card in the catalog that refers from a name or subject that is not used to one that is, from nothing to something.

Series entry: A card in the catalog for the series, a name under which different books (which may or may not be related) are sometimes published.

Shelf list: A list of books arranged according to the way the material appears on the shelf; usually copies of the main-entry catalog cards with accession numbers added to show how many copies are in the library collection.

Spine: The part of the book binding which conceals the sewn or bound edges of the pages, usually bearing the title and author's name; the part of the book that is visible when lined up side by side on a shelf.

Sub-title: The explanatory part of a title that in some cases follows the main title.

Subject heading: A word or group of words representing a subject under which cards on material dealing with that subject are filed in the catalog.

Table of contents: A listing of the chapters or sections in a book that usually appears near the front of the book after the title page.

Title page: A page at or near the beginning of a book on which is printed the title, author, place of publication and publisher.

Tracing: A record, usually on the main-entry card, of all the additional headings under which the item is represented in the catalog; a list of the added entries.

Vertical file: A file that stands upright, such as a standard office filing cabinet, which usually houses pamphlets, clippings, maps, etc., filed by subject topics.

Abbreviations

Abridged	abr.
Arranged	arr.
Association	assoc.
Black and white	b&w
Color	col.
Company	co.
Compiler	comp.
Copyright	c.
Corporation	corp.
Department	dept.
Document	doc.
Edition, editor	ed.
Enlarged	enl.
Frames	fr.
Government	govt.
Illustrations, illustrator	illus.
Inches	in.
Inches per second	ips.
Incorporated	inc.
Introduction	intro.
Joint author	jt. auth.
Limited	ltd.
Millimeters	mm.
Minutes	min.
Monaural	mono.
No date	n.d.
Number(s)	no.(s)
Page(s)	p.
.Part(s)	pt.(s)
Photographs	photos.
Plates	pl.
Preface	pref.
Pseudonym	pseud.
Revised	rev.
Second	sec.
Series	ser.

Session	sess.
Side	s.
Silent	si.
Sound	Sd.
Supplement	suppl.
Stereophonic	stereo.
Translator	tr.
United States	U.S.
Volume(s)	v.

The Dewey 200 Class

The first three subdivisions of the Dewey 200 - RELIGION class are as follows:

200 - RELIGION (general works)

    201 - PHILOSOPHY, THEORIES

    202 - HANDBOOKS AND OUTLINES

    203 - DICTIONARIES AND ENCYCLOPEDIAS

    204 - ESSAYS AND LECTURES

    205 - PERIODICALS

    206 - ORGANIZATIONS AND SOCIETIES

    207 - STUDY AND TEACHING (seminaries, etc.)

    208 - COLLECTIONS

    209 - HISTORY OF RELIGION

210 - NATURAL THEOLOGY

    211 - DEISM, ATHEISM, THEISM

    212 - PANTHEISM, THEOSOPHY

    213 - CREATION

    214 - THEODICY

    215 - RELIGION AND SCIENCE

    216 - GOOD AND EVIL, DEPRAVITY

    217 - WORSHIP, PRAYER (philosophy of)

    218 - IMMORTALITY, ETERNITY

    219 - ANALOGY

220 - BIBLE

    221 - OLD TESTAMENT

222 - HISTORICAL BOOKS

223 - POETIC BOOKS

224 - PROPHETIC BOOKS

225 - NEW TESTAMENT

226 - GOSPELS AND ACTS

227 - EPISTLES

228 - APOCALYPSE, REVELATION

229 - APOCRYPHA AND PSEUDEPIGRAPHA

230 - SYSTEMATIC OR DOCTRINAL THEOLOGY

231 - GOD

232 - JESUS CHRIST, CHRISTOLOGY

233 - MAN

234 - SOTERIOLOGY

235 - SAINTS, ANGELS, DEVILS

236 - ESCHATOLOGY

237 - FUTURE LIFE

238 - STATEMENT OF FUNDAMENTAL RELIGIOUS BELIEF

239 - APOLOGETICS

240 - DEVOTIONAL THEOLOGY

241 - MORAL THEOLOGY

242 - MEDITATION

243 - EVANGELISTIC WRITINGS

244 - STORIES, ALLEGORIES, SATIRES

245 - HYMNOLOGY

246 - CHRISTIAN SYMBOLISM

247 - ESTHETICS IN THE CHURCH

248 - PERSONAL RELIGION

249 - FAMILY DEVOTIONS

250 - PASTORAL THEOLOGY

    251 - HOMILETICS

    252 - SERMONS

    253 - PASTOR

    254 - CHURCH ADMINISTRATION

    255 - BROTHERHOODS, SISTERHOODS

    256 - SOCIETIES FOR PARISH WORK

    257 - PARISH EDUCATIONAL WORK

    258 - SOCIAL WELFARE WORK OF CHURCH

    259 - GROUP ORGANIZATIONS AND LEADERSHIP

260 - ECCLESIASTICAL THEOLOGY

    261 - CHRISTIAN SOCIAL THEOLOGY

    262 - CHURCH GOVERNMENT

    263 - CHRISTIAN SABBATH

    264 - PUBLIC WORSHIP

    265 - SACRAMENTS

    266 - MISSIONS

    267 - ASSOCIATIONS

    268 - CHURCH SCHOOLS, RELIGIOUS EDUCATION

    269 - REVIVALS, RETREATS, PARISH MISSIONS

270 GENERAL HISTORY OF THE CHRISTIAN CHURCH

    271 - RELIGIOUS ORDERS

    272 - PERSECUTIONS OF CHRISTIANS

    273 - HERESIES

274 - GENERAL CHURCH HISTORY OF EUROPE

275 - GENERAL CHURCH HISTORY OF ASIA

276 - GENERAL CHURCH HISTORY OF AFRICA

277 - GENERAL CHURCH HISTORY OF NORTH AMERICA

278 - GENERAL CHURCH HISTORY OF SOUTH AMERICA

279 - GENERAL CHURCH HISTORY OF OCEANIA, POLAR REGIONS

280 - CHRISTIAN CHURCHES AND SECTS

281 - PRIMITIVE AND ORIENTAL CHURCHES

282 - ROMAN CATHOLIC CHURCH

283 - ANGLICAN AND AMERICAN PROTESTANT EPISCOPAL CHURCH

284 - PROTESTANTISM

285 - PRESBYTERIAN, REFORMED, CONGREGATIONAL

286 - BAPTIST, IMMERSIONIST

287 - METHODIST

288 - UNITARIAN

289 - OTHER CHRISTIAN SECTS

290 - NON-CHRISTIAN RELIGIONS

291 - COMPARATIVE AND GENERAL MYTHOLOGY

292 - GREEK AND ROMAN RELIGION AND MYTHOLOGY

293 - TEUTONIC AND NORTHERN RELIGION AND MYTHOLOGY

294 - BUDDHISM, BRAHMANISM, HINDUISM

295 - NON-SEMITIC ASIATIC RELIGIONS

296 - JUDAISM

297 - MOHAMMEDANISM

298 -

299 - OTHER NON-CHRISTIAN RELIGIONS

Medium Designators

Designator	More Specific	Symbol*
BANNER		Ban
DIORAMA		Diorama
FILMSTRIP		FS
	FILMSLIP	FS
	SOUND FILMSTRIP	SFS
GAME		Game
GLOBE		Globe
KIT		K
MAP		Map
	CHART	Map
	RELIEF MAP	Map
	WALL MAP	Map
MICROFORM		M
	APERTURE CARD	MA
	MICROFICHE	MF
	MICROFILM REEL	MR
	MICROFILM CARTRIDGE	MC
	MICROFILM CASSETTE	MC
	MICRO-OPAQUE	MO
MODEL		Mod
MOTION PICTURE (FILM)		MP or F
	MOTION-PICTURE LOOP	MP or F
MUSIC		MS

*In all cases, the spelled-out word(s) may be used instead of a symbol.

	MUSICAL SCORE	MS
PERIODICAL		Per
PICTURE		PF or Pic
	ART PRINT	PF or Pic
	STUDY PRINT	PF or Pic
REALIA		Realia
RECORD		R or Rec
	RECORD ALBUM	R, Rec or RA
SLIDE		SL
	SLIDESET	SL
	AUDIOSLIDE	SL
	LANTERN SLIDE	SL
	STEREOSCOPE SLIDE	SL
TAPE		T
	TAPE CARTRIDGE	TC or Car
	TAPE CASSETTE	TC or Car
	TAPE REEL	TR or RRT
VERTICAL FILE		VF
	FLANNELGRAPH	VF
	FLASHCARD	VF
	FLIP CHART	VF or Map
	NEWSPAPER CLIPPING	VF
VIDEORECORDING		VR
	VIDEOTAPE RECORDING	VTR
	VIDEODISC RECORDING	VDR

Resources

Abridged Dewey Decimal Classification and Relative Index, by Melvil Dewey. 10th ed. Albany, NY, Forest Press, 1971.

Akers Simple Library Cataloging, completely revised and rewritten by Arthur Curley and Jana Varlejs. 6th ed. Metuchen, NJ, Scarecrow Press, 1977.

ALA Rules for Filing Catalog Cards, 2nd ed., abridged. Chicago, IL, American Library Association, 1968.

American Book Publishing Record (periodical). New York, NY, R.R. Bowker Co., monthly.

Audio-Visual Materials in the Church Library; How to Select, Catalog, Process, Store, Circulate, and Promote. Riverdale, MD, Church Library Council, 1977. (Available from author, 5406 Quintana Street, Riverdale, MD 20840.)

The Card Catalog (tape recording). Charles Burke, Box 494, Westport, CT 06880.

Cataloging and Classifying Media. Special Issue, Catholic Library World, v. 48, no. 10, May/June 1977.

Cataloging Books Step by Step, by Ruth S. Smith. Bryn Mawr, PA, Church and Synagogue Library Association, 1977.

Cataloging Manual for Nonbook Materials in Learning Centers and Libraries, by Judith Loveys Westhuis and Julia M. DeYoung. Rev. ed. Ann

Arbor, MI, Michigan Association of School Libraries, 1967. (Available from MASL, Publications Distribution Service, 615 East University, University of Michigan, Ann Arbor, MI 48106.)

Catholic Subject Headings, edited by Oliver L. Kaspner. 5th ed. Collegeville, MN, Liturgical Press, 1963.

Church Librarians Workbook. Minneapolis, MN, Lutheran Church Library Association, no date.

Church Library Manual, by Charlotte Newton. Author, 892 Prince Avenue, Athens GA, 1964.

The Church Library; Tips and Tools, by Gladys E. Scheer. St. Louis, MO, Bethany Press, 1973.

The Church Resource Library; How to Start It and Make it Grow by Maryann J. Dotts. Nashville, TN, Abingdon Press, 1976.

Classifying Library Materials, by Dorothy B. Kersten. Bryn Mawr, PA, Church and Synagogue Library Association, 1977.

Commonsense Cataloging; A Manual for the Organization of Book and Other Materials in School and Small Public Libraries, by Esther J. Piercy. Bronx, NY, H. W. Wilson Co., 1965.

Developing Multi-Media Libraries, by Warren B. Hicks and Alma M. Tillin. New York, NY, R. R. Bowker Co., 1970.

From Box to Bookshelf; A Handbook for Elementary Teacher-Librarians. St. Louis, MO, Concordia Publishing House, 1962.

Guide for the Organization and Operation of a Religious Resource Center, edited by John T. Corrigan. Haverford, PA, Catholic Library Association, 1977.

How to Build a Church Library, by Christine Buder. St. Louis, MO, Bethany Press, 1955.

How to Classify, Catalog and Maintain Media, by Jacqulyn Anderson. Nashville, TN, Broadman Press, 1978.

How to Process Media, by Jacqulyn Anderson. Nashville, TN, Broadman Press, 1978.

How to Organize and Operate a Small Library, by Genore H. Bernhard. Fort Atkinson, WI, Highsmith Company, 1975.

The Key to a Successful Church Library, by Erwin E. John. Minneapolis, MN, Augsburg Publishing House, 1958.

Leikind Classification System, by Miriam Leikind. The author, The Temple, University Circle at Silver Park, Cleveland, OH 44106.

Library Skills; Teaching Library Use Through Games and Devices, by School Library Association of California (Northern Section). Palo Alto, CA, Fearon Publishers, 1958.

Media Center Techniques Series (tape cassettes), by Jacqulyn Anderson. Nashville, TN, Broadman Press, 1978. (Contains four cassettes: "Classifying Books," "Cataloging Materials," "Subject Cataloging," and "Making and Using Cross-References." Available separately or as a set.)

Non-Book Materials; The Organization of Integrated Collections by Jane
Riddle, Shirley Lewis and Janet Macdonald. Ottawa, Canadian Library
Association, 1970.

The Organization of Books and Other Materials in School and Small Public
Library, revised by Marian Sanner. 2nd ed. Bronx, NY, H. W. Wilson
Company, 1974.

Relative Index to the Weine Classification Scheme for Judaica Libraries,
by Anita Loeb. Philadelphia, PA, Synagogue, School and Center Division,
Association of Jewish Libraries, 1972.

School Library Media Center Procedures, by Alma M. Tillin. Madison,
WI, Demco Library Supplies, 1973.

Sears List of Subject Headings, edited by Barbara M. Westby. 10th ed.
Bronx, NY, H. W. Wilson Company, 1977.

Simplified Cataloging Manual for Small Libraries and Private Collections.
San Jose, CA, Bibliographic Research Library, 1975.

Steps to Service; A Handbook of Procedures for the School Library Media
Center, by Mildred L. Nickel. Chicago, IL, American Library Association,
1975.

Subject Headings for Church or Synagogue Libraries, by Dorothy Kersten.
Bryn Mawr, PA, Church and Synagogue Library Association, 1978.

The Synagogue Library; Organization/Administration. New York, Library
Service Bureau, United Synagogue of America, 1968.

252

<u>200 (Religion) Class, Dewey Decimal Classification</u>. Nashville, TN,
Broadman Press, 1966.

<u>Weine Classification Scheme for Judaica Libraries</u>, by May Weine. 6th
ed. Philadelphia, PA, Synagogue, School and Center Division, Association of Jewish Libraries, 1975.

Index

Bound with: sample cards, 116
Bringing order out of chaos. See Screening materials
Bro-Dart, Inc.: address, 56
Browsing, 11-12, 24, 34
Buder, Christine, 71
Building the catalog, 3-4, 104-8
Burke Avenue Chapel, Seattle, WA, 46

Call number, 34-36, 95-96, 101-3, 112. See also types of media, i.e.,
    Musical scores
Card catalog, 39
Card catalog cabinet, 43-44, 70-71
Card set. See Catalog cards, set
Cardinal McClosky High School, Slingerland, NY, 218
Carpenter, Juanita, 100, 107, 224
Cartridges. See Tapes; Videotapes
Cassettes. See Tapes; Videotapes
Catalog, 2, 38; arrangement, 43-44; format, 38-40
Catalog cards, 43, 55, 57-58, 112; elements of information, 92; preparation,
    110-29, 152-55; set, 111; supplies, 64-65. See also types of media,
    i.e., Pictures
Catalog guide cards. See Guide cards
Cataloger, 20, 44-50, 225-26; basic requirements, 45-46
Cataloging Books Step By Step: reference, 52-53
Cataloging-in-publication, 99-100, 138-139
Celnik, Max, 71
Changes title. See Title change
Charging tray, 72
Children's Book Council, Inc.: address, 218
Children's books. See Juvenile books
Christ Episcopal Church, Oil City, PA, 48
Christian Board of Publication: address, 58
Church and Synagogue Libraries: reference, 146
Church and Synagogue Library Association (CSLA), 7, 21, 38, 49, 50, 52, 146;
    Library Services Committee, 79, 130
Church Library Council, 49, 59
Circulation records, 62-63
Class visits to library, 220
Classification, 8, 11-12; aids, 21, 99-101; methods, 12-24, 41, 97-99
Classification schemes. See Classification, methods
Classification symbols. See Call numbers
Classifying. See Classification, methods
Classifying Church or Synagogue Library Materials: reference, 21
Clippings, 148, 150; sample cards, 154
Cokesbury: address, 58; catalog, 4
Color-coded Dewey, 29-31
Color: use of, 29-32, 70-71
Coloring books, 222
Commercial processing services. See Processing services
Commonsense Cataloging: reference, 135
Compilation: sample card, 119

256

Compiler, 94; sample cards, 119, 126
Compound names: sample card, 114
Computers: use of, 39, 146-47
Conferences, congresses, meetings, etc.: sample card, 118
Consumer Information Catalog: reference, 148
Consumer Information Center: address, 148
Contents note: sample cards, 117, 122, 127. See also types of media,
     i.e., Records
Cooperative arrangements, 39; for cataloging, 39, 51-52; for ordering, 59
Copyright date, 96
Cornwell, Maxime, 222
Corporate author: sample card, 117
Correspondence courses, 7, 50
Cover title, 93; sample card, 121
Cox, Sylvia, 26
Cross references, 105, 151-52, 217
Curley, Arthur, 94, 135
Cutter number tables, 35, 102

Date: choice of, 96
Date of publication, 96, 112
Date slips, 55, 57-58, 66
Dater, 58
Decimal classification. See Dewey decimal classification
Demo Educational Corporation: address, 56; Library Supplies, 76
Demonstrating use of the catalog, 1-4, 213-14, 219
Denominational library services, 58
Dewey decimal classification, 12, 14, 49, 97, 99-100; defined, 15-19;
     variations, 19-21, 24, 29-31, 107
Dictionary catalog. See Integrated catalog
Dietz, Mrs. Edith, 46
Dioramas, 204-5; sample card, 204
Directions for users. See Signs; Guide cards; Leaflet of instructions
Displays, 218
Divided catalog, 44
Dividing the work. See Staff
Documenting the procedures. See Procedures manuals
Dotts, Maryann J., 14, 51
Drew, Mrs. C. B., 13
Duke Hospital Library, 84
Dummy markets, 137
Dust Jackets. See Jacket covers

Edition, 94-95, 114; sample cards, 115-16, 118-19, 125
Editor, 94; sample cards, 116, 118, 121, 125, 130
Electric pencil. See Stylus, electric
Elements of information, 91-92
Eraser, 74-75

Training, 6-7, 50
Transfer paper, 35, 57, 69
Transparencies, 184-86; sample cards, 185-86
Translator, 94, 113; sample cards, 117, 125
200 RELIGION Class, Dewey Decimal Classification: reference, 21
Typing, 47, 109-12, 123-34, 129-31, 151-54

Ulland, Rose Mary, 170
UNICEF, 31
Uniform title, 195
United Methodist Church, Church Library Service, address, 50
University of Pittsburgh, 105
University of the Pacific, 106
University of Utah, 7, 50

Varlejs, Jana, 93, 135
Vertical file, 148-54, 162-64; sample cards, 152-54
Videotape recordings, 178-80; sample cards, 179-80
Visits to classrooms, 220
Volumes in set, 96, 113; sample cards, 117, 130

Wallace, Shari, 220
Washington Hebrew Congregation, Washington, DC, 40
Webster, Stewart H., 193
Weeding, 79-80, 224-25
Weine, Mae, 24
Weine classification, 24
Westby, Barbara M., 21
White, Joyce L., 29, 38
Withdrawals. See Weeding
Withdrawn file, 225
Work cabinet, 48
Work card, 47, 90-91, 97, 99, 102-4; sample card, 91
Workshops, conferences and courses. See Training

Xerox Bibliographics, address, 142